The story of rope making has often been a footnote to history; a process whose modest ubiquity has denied it a prominent place in the story of Britain's Industrial Revolution. However, in Barton-upon-Humber, Hall's Barton Ropery Co. Ltd. touched the lives of generations of workers and placed an ancient rural craft in the forefront of Barton's industrial development. Such an important transformation never passed unnoticed in Barton, and the first complete history of the firm was published by Hall's in 1924.[1] Subsequently updated in 1974, this latest edition has become accepted as the story of Hall's Barton Ropery, and stands to this day as the epitaph of the firm.[2] In 2007, we have assessed, considered and re-presented this story with the hope that the role of Hall's Barton Ropery shall never become a footnote to the history of Barton-upon-Humber.

To say that the origins of rope making are lost in antiquity is probably accurate. Various sources suggest 'modern' rope making techniques were established in Egypt by 3000BC, and similar ropes are still produced in rural Egypt today.[3] In Britain, it is likely that from Prehistoric times, ropes were produced using lime tree bark, grasses and even the (surprisingly strong) stem of the stinging nettle.[4] Rope making emerged as a skilled occupation during the Roman period, and by the time of the Norman Conquest 'Roper' was a common English surname.[5] Evidence for rope makers working as part of wider rural industry exists in Lincolnshire from the fourteenth century, and by the sixteenth century the county held a firm reputation for cultivating hemp and flax on a large scale.[6] The first detailed reference to rope making in Barton is contained in the 1676 'Town Book'. Recording the customs and obligations of Barton's inhabitants to Church and Manor, it perhaps represents centuries of accumulated practices, and demonstrates that the growing of hemp was firmly established in Barton's economy well before the seventeenth century.[7]

Traditionally, the date given for the foundation of Hall's Ropery is 1767. It is probable that this was the initial move by William Hall into the business of rope making, rather than any concerted effort to build a rope making 'factory' at Barton. The Hall family were successful merchants and ship owners, securing great wealth from trading to Baltic and European ports. It is likely that the Hall family's Baltic trade links complemented their new rope making interests, as the importation of Russian hemp became common for rope making during the eighteenth century.[8] Before the nineteenth century, rope making in Barton represented only a small (but increasingly important) part of the Hall family's interests.[9]

John Hall (1775-1863). The father of Hall's Ropery

The foundation of a 'modern' rope works, with permanent buildings and the characteristic 'walk' occurred sometime between 1800 and 1803 when Thomas Hall and his son William purchased land on the east side of Barton's Haven.[10] Almost immediately, and certainly by 1802, the business and land was transferred to John Hall, Thomas's eldest son and William's brother. Born in 1775, John was still a young man, but one with a wealth of nautical and trading experience.[11] Having become the successful master of one of the family's ships in 1796 he was willing to explore markets not usually exploited by Hull's merchants, such as those in the West Indies. However, his main trading links focused on the Baltic ports, and along with many other members of Hull's merchant community, he was quick to exploit the growing whaling industry. In 1804, one of John's ships brought home a record whaling catch, which was never surpassed in the forty or so years the industry remained active in Hull.[12]

It was John Hall who began the development of rope making in earnest, and in 1808 he filed a patent for an improvement in the process.[13] This was during a period in which technological innovation in rope making was developing quickly, and technical pioneers were becoming very wealthy men. Throughout his lifetime John invested capital in the rope works, and aligned his shipping interests to serve it. Indeed, in 1852 it was noted in the *Stamford Mercury* (in one of the few instances when the rope works is mentioned) that John Hall had undertaken to deepen the Haven so as to let boats unload easier at his works.[14] As the nineteenth century progressed, the rope works expanded steadily. Gas lighting was introduced, and sometime before 1851, steam power was first used at the site.[15] This development did not go unnoticed by the first generation of Barton's historians, such as Charles Henry Ball and William Hesleden, who mentioned the rope works in their accounts of the town written during the 1850s.[16] In no uncertain terms they ascribed the rope works the role of both major employer, technical innovator, and importantly, a main factor in the development of Barton as an industrial town.

Captain J. Huddart (1741 - 1816) revolutionised ropemaking when he invented this machine in 1793. Following his technological lead could reap great financial rewards.

Despite increasing financial involvement in Barton, it seems likely that John Hall was content to live in Hull and Sculcoates throughout his life; there is no evidence that he built any house in Barton.[17] John Hall died in Baker Street, Hull in 1863. His son, John Edward, was the first member of the Hall family to run the factory from Barton itself. It was John Edward who built a large house adjacent to the rope works during the later 1850s, before his first son was born and baptised in Barton in 1861. He remained in charge until the company was reformed in 1890. John Edward Hall, with none of the romance of sea-faring and 'adventuring' traditionally associated with his father, has been somewhat overlooked by historians of the firm. Left a company worth around £9,000 by his father, John Edward Hall ensured Hall's Ropery expanded greatly during his tenure, especially in regard to the development of steam power for making ropes.[18] It appears the company was very successful under his leadership, and as he was living within Barton it was noted that his management style was different from that of his father, taking a much closer interest in the day-to-day running of the works.[19] Yet he remains rather an enigma, appearing in few of the surviving sources for Barton's social and civic history. It is known that in 1864 John Edward financed the building of a Mission Church, built as part of the rope works buildings, and there are several documents which detail charitable donations to Hull Trinity House and various other charities.[20] However, this seems to represent the extent of his philanthropic and social engagement with the Barton community.

John Edward Hall (1827-1895) inherited Hall's Ropery from his father in 1863. The booming business was worth over £9,000.

Thomas Hall Sissons (1836-1920) substantially financed the reformed company and as the primary investor he became Chairman in 1890.

Few setbacks occurred in this period of prosperity, despite a fatality in 1855 and a flood in 1868 being noted in contemporary sources.[21] However, the later nineteenth century presented the company with many problems which lead to its near collapse in 1890. The ending of the age of sail saw demand for traditional rope rigging fall significantly, and the introduction of steel cable did nothing to help this trend. For a company that still relied so heavily on the shipping of Hull and Grimsby, the effects on the business were grave, and when combined with a generally poor national economic performance in the later 1880s, were nearly catastrophic.[22] The advent of steam fishing left many smaller fishing outfits completely redundant, and the company subsequently suffered heavily from bad debts during this period.[23]

So in 1890, Hall's Barton Ropery Co. Ltd. was created as a private limited company to raise enough capital to survive the troubles of the period, and was financed substantially by the Sissons family. The Sissons family was related to the Halls by marriage, and the new company chairman was Thomas Hall Sissons, primary investor and John Edward Hall's brother-in-law. Hall's Barton Ropery made it a priority to engage in wire rope manufacture, and began this in 1891.[24] No wire rope was actually produced on the 'old' Barton site, instead the company purchased Overton Brother's wire rope works in Beverley. The capital expenditure of £15,000 used to save the company was a substantial amount, but it seems this investment was not matched by a change in focus by the company, as by 1900, 50% of the company had to be sold to the Wilson Shipping Line of Hull.[25] This was attributed mainly to a continuing reluctance by the company to export their products. It is probable that the company contracted, as it is recorded that many of the company's ships were sold in 1891, leaving perhaps as few as two in its ownership throughout the 1890s. (In comparison, sixty years earlier, John Hall had built and registered four ships for use by the rope works).[26] The company then moved to offices in De La Pole House in Hull, a fine medieval town house. This was a proud asset but sadly became the last resting place of the company's archives which were destroyed by bombing during the Second World War.

In 1901 Arthur Hendy joined the company as cashier. He later became Managing Director, and his family name was associated with the works for the best part of the following century.[27]

Although no dividends were paid in the first few years of the new company's existence, recovery did eventually take place. The company probably benefited from the opening of Immingham docks in 1913, then the largest deep water dock in the United Kingdom, and a huge boost to the shipping economy of the Humber region.[28] The relatively new ports of Grimsby and Goole also continued to develop, and after surviving the difficulties of the great changes in the fishing industry which nearly closed the company, the ropery profited from the 'new' industrial scale fishing based there in the early twentieth century.[29]

During the first decades of the twentieth century, the company began to profit from the snowballing military build-up. As early as 1908 the company produced ropes designed to tow Dreadnought battleships. These were of up to forty inches in circumference, then the largest the company had produced.[30] During the Great War the company was a large producer of all kinds of rope for military use, and the Admiralty orders represented the watershed for the company's wire rope division. It became a prime national producer of steel guy-wires for aeroplane wings, and anti-submarine nets; both uses for steel wire essentially resulting from the needs of war.[31] Subsequently, in 1918 the company was in a strong position relative to other, smaller, rope manufacturers. In 1920 Thomas Hall Sissons died and was replaced as Chairman by Arthur Barton Hall, (as his name suggests, he was indeed the first member of the Hall family to be born in Barton!). He was the son of John Edward Hall. In 1921 much of the ropewalk was damaged by an unusually high tide, and the majority of the present building dates from the rebuilding that took place around 1922.[32] As part of this rebuilding openings were included in the walls of the ropewalk to enable any future floodwater to drain freely. These openings can be seen on the outside of the building today.

The wire rope division remained profitable throughout the troubled economic conditions of the early 1920s, but the natural-fibre works at Barton suffered to a much greater extent. No dividends were paid to shareholders in 1922 and the situation remained bleak throughout the 1920s.[33] The decline of the coal industry culminating in the general strike of 1926 had an immediate effect on the demand for ropes. As the full extent of the Great Depression became clear, it seems that the wire rope division was the company's salvation, offsetting the losses of around £10,000 that the Barton site suffered during the early 1930s. Indeed, by 1939 the wire rope works were producing four times as much material as they had in 1936.[34] A major contributory factor to the company's recovery was the re-armament immediately preceding the Second World War.[35] Following the declaration of war, production was controlled directly by the Admiralty and once again the company played a significant role in the war effort.

In the immediate post-war period the company was in a relatively strong position, but heavy taxation precluded any possibility of making much profit.[36] Roland Dagwell, who had joined the company in 1938 as Export Manager, returned from wartime service and continued to develop the company's overseas business. Dagwell must have realised the importance of foreign markets in a time when 'export or die' was the order of the day. When he became Managing Director in 1953, after the death of Arthur Hendy, he continued the development of foreign trade, especially creating links with the burgeoning heavy-industries in South America and the Middle East.[37] This coincided with the opening of new offices in Hull to replace those lost during the Second World War. Throughout the 1950s the business was stable, and foreign markets grew in importance; rope was in demand for all sorts of uses including oil drilling, mining, haulage and shipping. The company was compelled to invest in modern machinery and re-organised its storage systems to improve efficiency, although by far the most notable development was the adoption of synthetic rope making.

Synthetic fibres were to revolutionise rope making, being stronger, lighter, waterproof and cheaper to produce than natural ropes. Machinery to exploit synthetic rope production was built on the site of some older, by then redundant, processes at Barton, such as the production of 'tow' rope (poor quality rope re-manufactured from scraps). The development of synthetic fibres, beginning with polyester, moved with great pace and by 1960 synthetic fibres of modern standards were available.[38] Hall's found the production of synthetic rope profitable; evidence shows that much of the synthetic rope was used in 'everyday' applications where it replaced sisal and manila rope. The business contrived to ensure any rope could be available 'ex-stock' or at very short notice, sometimes a single working day.[39] This was an important policy enabling Hall's Barton Ropery to compete with manufacturers who possessed much greater resources. The company remained in the business of the production of natural fibre ropes, and it appears they aligned this aspect of the business to the fulfilling of specialist orders where the proven qualities of manila or sisal rope were sought over the lower price of synthetic ropes.[40] Indeed, as many other rope manufacturers contracted and closed, Hall's Barton Ropery remained one of the few rope manufacturers in the country that could produce ropes of unusual characteristics; in length, lay or quality. Certainly, large companies such as British Ropes tended to abandon such specialist rope in favour of the production of synthetic alternatives. Alas, it could be argued that Hall's could not compete with such large industrial combines and the decision to remain a 'specialist' rope maker was probably one made with little choice, eager to remain independent in a period when many smaller rope works were struggling. Those with fond memories of the company often recall the 'special' ropes the company made, and it has often been said that the ropes used on the first successful ascent of Everest were produced in Barton. Unfortunately, no documentary evidence remains of this achievement.[41] There were many orders from such unusual customers as the United States Navy who provided very detailed specifications and expectations of quality. Indeed, the company was keen to publicise its ability to produce unusually long lengths of rope, 'throwing open the doors and working outside' if necessary.[42]

The Management at Hall's Barton Ropery.

The company continued to be successful throughout the 1960s, Roland Dagwell becoming Chairman in 1962.[43] The company's success fitted well with the general success of all industry in the Humber region, notably in the emergent chemical, paint and oil industries. Rope making as an industry remained an important part of manufacturing in the area, accounting for 4.5% of the region's production in 1967, the bulk of which must have derived from Hall's Barton Ropery.[44] In the home markets the company relied heavily on orders from repeat customers, and state owned industries such as the British Coal Board, British Steel Corporation, British

Railways, and numerous other utility and shipping boards.[45] Modernisation of the works and its machinery carried on, and gained pace when Tom Nicholson became Work's Manager. Money was always a problem though, and during this period it was a constant struggle to keep the old ropewalk building weather proof. Eventually, and in line with national requirements regarding working conditions, the southern part of the walk, dating from the first decade of the nineteenth century, was rebuilt in metal and asbestos.

During the 1970s the area suffered greatly from economic recession. The attendant loss of many fisheries effectively brought to an end Hall's centuries-long association with the British maritime industry. New avenues were explored and Hall's Barton Ropery made a good name for itself in Icelandic and Canadian fishing markets.[46] Business was hard and Hall's found it increasingly difficult to maintain stock levels and therefore quick deliveries. Despite their struggle to remain independent, Hall's could not prevent Bridport-Gundry purchasing the company in 1986. Before Bridport-Gundry's long-term plans for Hall's Barton Ropery were revealed, the company was sold once again, to Bridon Plc, (formerly called British Ropes). The decision to close the Barton site was made immediately and, in December 1989, the works produced its last rope.[47] The buildings were stripped and machinery either broken up or sold to other manufacturers. Centuries of rope making in Barton had come to an end.

The Ropery Bell, in many ways the heart of the Rope Works, was rung to signal to men at the opposite end of the ropewalk, nearly ¹/₄ mile away, that a rope had been completed. When this photograph was taken in 1970 the southern reaches of the ropewalk had remained largely unchanged since the early nineteenth century.

photo - courtesy David Lee

1. Mr Hall's Ropery

This chapter will approach what has traditionally been a footnote in the history of Hall's Ropery; the circumstances of its birth. Although much is lost in the darkness of history, there is a surprising body of surviving evidence remaining. In many histories of the company it is simply stated that Hall's rope making enterprise was a 'natural' extension of their shipping activities.[1] It is the intention here to approach that assertion critically, and to attempt to understand the importance of wider economic and political factors which may have influenced Hall's decision to set up a rope making concern in Barton.

Like most rural communities, Barton people grew flax to provide for their own domestic needs. The town's ancient links to the River Humber and the sea beyond helped boost the local demand for rope and sailcloth, as did the large number of windmills that existed in this region. The production of flax and hemp is mentioned in the Barton Town Book of 1676, which clearly places its role at the heart of the parish's economy.[2] However, rope making in Barton did not (or rather could not) engage with wider markets. This stemmed mainly from the small-scale nature of the process. Inventories left by 'Ropers' during the seventeenth century show that few, if any, possessed any sort of machinery to help them increase production.[3] Indeed, illustrations dated 1802 show men spinning rope by hand, making it anywhere they could 'walk' the length required. Subsequently the early history of rope making in Barton has left historians and archaeologists with no firm evidence.

Early rope making was done by hand on any plot of land long enough to walk the desired length of the rope. W.H. Pyne sketched this view of ropemakers at work in his series featuring idyllic views of rural industry, 1808.

We do know, however, that Halls' first permanent and substantial rope making building was built at Barton some time between 1800 and 1806. This, for many, represents the beginning of industrial rope making in the town. But, the story of the Hall's Ropery begins much earlier, in the eighteenth century, in the nearby port of Hull. As the eighteenth century progressed, Hull was developing rapidly as a port of great significance; export trade had doubled between 1750 and 1780.[4] The merchants and traders of Hull were increasingly wealthy, and the Hall family almost certainly profited from the development of trade from the port.

The increase in shipping activity changed the nature of trading. The subsequent boom in shipping meant that ship owning and ship building became viable as separate commercial enterprises.[5] The cost of both these enterprises was particularly high, and fortunes could not be made quickly by ship owning alone. However, the shipping boom created a constant demand for sailcloth and rope. Because sailcloth manufacture, and to an even greater extent rope making, required much less capital than ship owning, investment in these industries provided a good business opportunity for men of more modest means.

The process of rope making had not changed; it was still not an industry in the conventional sense. To meet the new demands placed on it by Hull's expanding fleet it needed regimentation. And so in 1757, Haldenby-Dixon opened the first rope works in Hull; Standidge & Wright quickly followed.[6] The industry should have thrived, as Hull's Baltic links could be easily exploited to import flax in much greater quantities than could be grown locally. However, the earliest rope makers of Hull failed in their ventures, almost certainly because of a difficulty finding labourers. The development of Hull provided new opportunities for even the lowest class of labourer, and hemp spinning was seen as a poorly paid and an undesirable occupation for the majority of Hull's workers. Historians have used this initial failure of the rope industry to surmise that Thomas Hall located his initial venture of 1767 in Barton to secure a workforce more willing (or at least more desperately poor) than that in Hull.[7] If this was his reason, his judgement was vindicated. The presence of a rope making tradition in Barton before 1767 was almost certainly an important factor in Hall's decision to locate his enterprise there, as it provided him with a community which already possessed a collective expertise in rope making. This was important for the Halls, having come to the industry with no direct experience in rope making themselves. This raises the significant prospect that the Halls were pioneers of labour organisation, providing the essential beginnings for the later industrial revolution which Barton experienced.

Hall's Ropery, in its earliest years, was an important aspect of the family's business interests, but it does not appear to have been listed as a separate venture throughout the course of the eighteenth century.[8] It appears that the Halls remained primarily a shipping and trading family, developing profitable links with Baltic ports. It is impossible to define the connection between the Halls' trading activities and their rope making enterprise as no records survive. Although it is likely that Hall chose Barton as the location for his rope works because of extensive local hemp supplies, it is also possible that the family's shipping contacts with suppliers of hemp and flax in Russia and Scandinavia was an important factor in their desire to invest in rope making. The earliest written record of flax being imported into Barton from Russia is 1802, although it is probable that the Hall family, like others, had begun this process sometime before that date.[9] Conversely, the desire for Hall to maximise his profit from the Barton ropers may have contributed to the driving force behind the huge increase in imported hemp and flax handled by the port of Hull in the 1780s. It is entirely possible that Hall was directly influencing the region's embryonic industrial development by both organising the import of raw materials whilst also reorganising a workforce that had changed little in character since medieval times.

By the end of the eighteenth century the Halls' business interests had become widespread. There was, however, a small but increasingly important group of traders in Hull who specialised in particular industries. One of these was the Hassell family who as hemp traders are reported to have been associates of the Halls in the earlier eighteenth century.[10] Indeed, they may have been instrumental in facilitating Hall's success in his rope making enterprise through their extensive professional contacts in the hemp markets of Russia and the Baltic. The association with the Hassell family is well charted throughout the nineteenth century and was later reinforced by marriage.[11] The increasing demarcation of trades in the later eighteenth century was partly a reaction to the increasing capital investment needed by merchants. However, it was also partly a desire to consolidate business ventures that had been developed over several generations and were only then becoming profitable enough to pursue in isolation. The Hall family's eventual decision to focus on rope making at Barton may have been one of foresight, but a number of economic and, crucially, political factors may have coloured their judgement.

Perhaps the most important political factor was the effect of the Napoleonic War. As this progressed many continental ports were blockaded. Although Russian supplies of flax and hemp would not collapse until Russia entered the war on the side of the French in 1807, the overall effect before this date was to create a more volatile and greatly restricted trade.[12] The effect on the traders of Hull, who customarily had no West Indian, American or Asian trade to fall back on, was considerable. This fall in trade did present some opportunities as it was coupled with a rapid development of shipping, mainly for naval requirements. As general merchants Hall's were flexible enough to react to these rapid short-term changes in the market. Rope making and sailcloth manufacture was clearly an avenue of business which could prove to be profitable in the future. John Hall, Thomas's son and by now master of his father's ship *Aurora,* was adept at reacting to the changing political situation. Perhaps through his links to the maritime establishment at Trinity House, where his uncle was an Elder Brother, John made several contracts with the Admiralty to become a privateer.[13] The sole surviving record of John's privateering enterprise helps to illustrate the wealth he could have generated through this action.[14] However, John Hall found himself without a ship when the *Aurora* was lost in the Humber Estuary around 1810.[15]

The Aurora, built in Whitby in 1793, was captained by John Hall from 1795 until around 1810, when it was wrecked in the Humber Estuary.

As war raged in Europe, the seeds of Barton's industrial revolution were beginning to germinate. In 1793, the Parliamentary Act for the enclosure of Barton was passed. Surveying began soon after and all the new boundaries were completed in 1796.[16] A large area of land called the *Brick Closes*, immediately adjacent to the east bank of Barton Haven, was awarded to George and Sarah Uppleby.[17] This ideally situated land was considerably boosted in value by the construction, as part of the Enclosure Act, of stone jetties at the Haven and along the banks of the Humber.[18] So, when in June 1800, George Uppleby decided to sell the land it was advertised in the *Stamford Mercury* as:

'Exceedingly eligible for the building mills, warehouses or granaries, next to the public drain or haven, which is navigable to the Humber.'[19]

The agreement for the sale of this land survives and besides detailing the length of the plot, deliberately chosen as a long and narrow stretch of land for the purpose of rope walking, it also details the names of the purchasers. Thomas and William Hall, father and son, along with Thomas Murdock, took possession of a third each, paying a total of £898.[20] Whilst both the

Halls are noted as being residents of Hull, William Murdock was described as a Roper 'of Barton'. Whether or not the partnership was forged prior to this 1800 agreement, it is clear that the Halls were eager to invest in a rope making concern which was already well developed in terms of expertise if not capital. To reinforce this, another early partner in the firm, William Burton, had spent many years working for Spyvee & Cooper, the premier rope makers of Hull.[21]   Once again the historian is drawn to conclude that Halls' main aim in opening the enterprise in Barton was one mainly of labour organisation, rather than 'clean sheet' industrial speculation. The implications of the Murdock-Hall-Burton partnership are important, not least as it is probably the first tangible evidence of any industry in the Humber falling under direct control of men based in the port and financial centre of Hull. Historians have commented on the willingness of Hull merchants to trade with 'all the smallest creeks and havens', but have emphasised the small-scale (and essentially ancient) nature of this trade.[22]

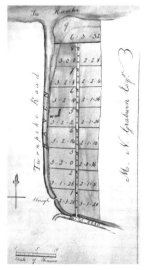

This nineteenth century sketch shows the parcels of land which were purchased by Hall's and Burton to build their ropewalk. The boundaries drawn in this agreement can still be identified today.

The Halls' forging of formal trade links with Barton is clear evidence that Hull merchants were beginning to realise the potential locked in the city's hinterland, a potential visible beyond the short term needs placed on trade by the Napoleonic War. Murdock left the partnership early in 1803, but Burton continued to help run the works until his death in the mid 1830s.[23]   The sole surviving page of a company day-book shows Burton was well paid for his management of the company. In one month in 1802 he was paid ten pounds. At this date it would be unusual for a skilled labourer, assuming he remained employed for a full 52 weeks, to earn £25 in one year.[24]

When John Hall inherited the ropewalk at Barton in 1802, he was aged just 27.

In 1801, perhaps with few if any buildings situated on the new site, the business was transferred to John Hall, Thomas's son. It is likely that John began the development of industrial-scale rope making on the present site. There is evidence to suggest that John Hall was increasingly attracted to running the rope works himself. For instance, in 1804 when John's ship the *Aurora* brought home a record catch of whale oil, John did not captain the ship himself.[25] These long expeditions, which he undertook personally during the eighteenth century, were now too time-consuming if he was to develop his land-based interests. In 1808, John Hall filed a patent for new methods of coiling lines, which illustrates his desire to introduce the most modern technology to the rope works.[26] This occurred at a time when technological solutions were being aimed at traditional industries. Pioneers such as Captain J. Huddart developed many new techniques to improve the strength and durability of ropes in the first decade of the nineteenth century, and subsequently profited immensely from their endeavours. Huddart's London-Limehouse Ropery became one of the largest in the country.[27] Importantly then, John Hall's rope-coiling patent was explicitly aimed at the needs of the Admiralty, thus emulating the efforts of the now-famous Capt. Huddart. The connection with the Admiralty was shared by many members of his family. Francis, John's uncle, had volunteered in 1802 to provide his ship for patrolling the Humber when a French invasion was threatened.[28] Such Admiralty links were perhaps a major motivating factor in the development of the rope works. John Hall's business records no longer survive, but it is commonly written that the company produced 'considerable government stores' at Barton.[29] As the Napoleonic War and its destruction of shipping by armed vessels showed little sign of ending, it is possible that John Hall felt the production of supplies for the Admiralty was a much safer enterprise, both financially and physically. John Hall's rope-coiling patent represents a watershed in the development of rope making at Barton. Alas, the new technique did not alter the production method substantially and horses were still the main power source at the works. Despite this however, the patent demonstrated some of the first attempts by members of the Hall family to take direct control of the physical process of rope making at Barton. This was a marked change from the period in which the family seemed content to organise the business around the ability of Barton rope makers to work as they had done for centuries with little or no direct involvement.

An early business card for John Hall's new Ropery. c1810.

Yet John Hall did not abandon his other trading interests; instead it seems that he gradually began to realign them to the needs of his new rope works. Histories of the firm, written before records were lost, give some detail about John Hall's trading. He continued to import flax and hemp which became the core of his trading activity after which forays to the West Indies were merely profitable diversions.[30] Hall's ship-owning interests began to work more closely with his rope making activities in Barton. From 1806 he took part-ownership of a number of ships with his partner William Burton. These ships, registered at Barton rather than Hull, go some way to support the suggestion that John Hall was aligning his other interests to serve his rope making business. Many of these ships were likely to have engaged in the transfer of flax and hemp from larger ships docked in Hull and brought across the river to Barton for processing. The relatively large number of ships owned by the Hall-Murdock-Burton partnership in the early nineteenth century illustrates the decreasing importance of locally grown flax and hemp. Throughout this period, personal contacts were key to successful business, and the extended Hall family served John well. For instance, as part owner of the schooner *Mary-Ann* with a Francis Hall of South Shields, John ensured strong links with other important markets, securing a future for the company beyond the local needs of Barton and the estuary.[31]

The Ropery's strong links with Hull were established before the end of the Napoleonic War. When there was a fire at the works in 1807, the subsequent reconstruction (of which the 'Despatch Building' still stands) was substantial and reflected the increased capital Hall was prepared to invest in the company. Indeed, around 1829 a steam engine was introduced to replace horse-power for spinning ropes. The use of a steam engine was a significant development in the evolution of rope making and was one of the first departures from the traditional process. The installation of steam power was roughly contemporary with the introduction of similar machinery in other rope making concerns across the country, but is notable in Barton because of its smaller scale when compared for instance with the Gourock rope works in Glasgow.[32] The considerable capital investment that was needed to purchase a steam engine suggests the company was very successful, but it is possible that John Hall's income from his shipping interests provided him with the necessary funds. Throughout his life he was prepared to engage in speculative shipping ventures, being involved in the embryonic East Indies and growing US trades. The company's historians have been eager to mention his willingness to send ships to Australia, to ship unusual goods such as pearls, and to continue profiting from the conditions in wartime by running guns for the Confederate States during the American Civil War. However John Hall secured the means to install steam power, it must have increased his capacity greatly, but more importantly it shows his willingness to invest in the Barton site. It is arguably this initial investment that allowed Hall's Ropery to become premier rope makers, and eventually a company with international significance.

The Despatch Building is the oldest part of the ropewalk still standing, and dates from 1807. It was used to store finished rope before it was loaded on to vessels bound for markets in Hull and beyond.

photo - Brian Peeps

2. "Every description of cordage"

When, in 1856, Henry Wm. Ball sat to write his history of Barton, using the collected notes of William Hesleden, he described a town proud of its ancient past, but equally aware of the great changes the first half of the century had brought. Ball's commentary is interesting and although firmly of the antiquarian school of history, can nevertheless be used by the modern historian as an interesting route into understanding Barton at the mid-century. The brief mention of the rope works amounts to no more than eight lines, yet the significance of its inclusion belies Ball's brevity as the historian is presented with an approximation of the scale of the enterprise. Ball reports the 'average number of hands employed' as numbering 100.[1] Even more important is the evidence that shows how the rope works fitted into the social consciousness of Barton. Ball's language implies a certain sense of collective pride that a company in Barton had manufactured 'immense government stores' and produced 'every description of cordage'.[2] In fact, on a more fundamental level, it is perhaps also significant that 'Mr. Hall's Ropery' is mentioned by name when at least three other major rope manufacturers that operated in Barton during this period pass without mention. Ball places his description in a discourse focussing on a burgeoning industrial economy, describing whiting mills, tanning yards and, most prominently, Barton's brick and tile manufactories. Therefore this chapter aims to look further into how the rope works contributed to the birth of an 'industrial Barton'.

At this point it may be illuminating to consider what Ball saw when he observed Hall's works in 1856. Of course, little documentary or archaeological evidence survives, but through a synthesis of a wide range of sources, it is possible to create a general impression of Hall's rope 'factory' as it appeared fifty years into its existence. The whole site consisted of a modest collection of brick buildings bounded by the Haven on its west side.[3] Many of the work's buildings were carefully protected to prevent the spread of fire; the tar sheds and hemp stores being free-standing for this purpose.[4] The hemp store would also have been lined with wood and well weather-proofed to prevent the rotting of the raw materials it contained.[5] There was a large room for hatchelling, or the hand-preparation of fibres. Adjoined to this would be room for the spinning of hemp into yarn, although this could have been continued outdoors at this time. Nearby would have stood a brick boiler house and steam engine and, attached to this, a form of 'mill' housing some basic steam-powered machinery for the making of ropes. Somewhere on the site would be workshops and a further small mill for the production of sailcloth. In the whole, these buildings clustered around the south end of the site, with two brick cottages housing the rope works managers (but not John Hall himself).[6] The ropewalk itself possessed a tiled roof, even if its sides were not built of brick for its full length. Given the costal location of the site it is not unreasonable to conjecture that some form of siding was attached to the walk, or that a brick-built structure was not conceived from the beginning. Ropewalks often possessed rudimentary wooden siding to prevent the worst of the weather encroaching on the interior.[7] The whole site covered roughly fifteen acres, and it was reported in 1856 that it was lit by gas; John Hall being a minor shareholder in Barton's newly formed Gas Company.[8]

A plan of Barton 'Waterside' showing the rope works. A detail from the 1855 (upside down) map of Barton.

Contemporary mention of the rope works names it as Mr Hall's Ropery, and indeed it is tempting for us to focus our efforts on the life and times of the rather colourful character, John Hall.[9] The preceding chapter was indeed as much the story of the Hall family as it was a history of the town of Barton, or even the history of rope making. This chapter will examine the role of those who worked in the rope works, and their contribution to the development of Barton. Who were they? Where did they come from? Where did they live? And what jobs did they do?

We must first consider the most historically 'visible' effects of the rope works. The rope works had a very important effect on the population of Barton throughout the nineteenth century, and as discussed in the previous chapter, it is probable that Thomas Hall sited his ropery concern in Barton in order to exploit an existing workforce.[10] With closer study of the nineteenth century censuses it becomes increasingly obvious that by the time the first detailed census information is available many ropers were coming from outside Barton. The extract below is from the 1861 census.

Name	Position	Age	Occupation	Place of Birth
John Graves	Head	38	Ropemaker	Scotland
Martha	Wife	37	-	Scotland
Jayne	Daughter	11	-	Scotland
John	Son	8	-	Scotland
William	Son	7	-	Scotland
Mary	Daughter	5	-	Scotland
1861 Census, Barton-Upon-Humber, St. Peter's Parish, Ropery Houses.				

The example of John Graves' family is a common one, for when the birthplaces of those in the general populace are compared with ropers, the difference is especially noticeable: around 62% of all ropers were born outside the parish compared to 51% of the adult population as a whole.[11] Of course these figures are difficult to penetrate further, not least because of the rather haphazard recording of occupations during the nineteenth century. Nevertheless, it is clear that many of those who had migrated to Barton, and in 1851 found themselves working at the rope works, had arrived in the town as early as the first decade of the nineteenth century. It is a leap of great historical faith to suggest that Barton actually attracted rope makers specifically, but the arrival of John Graves may well be evidence of this. Barton's building boom was probably fuelled by such migrant workers rather than any increased demand through the natural increase of the established population. Certainly the Ropery Houses, where the Graves family were living, were built as part of the rope works sometime during the mid 1850s.

In contrast, the following examples serve to illustrate how, at the opposite end of the labour 'market', it appeared that journeymen workers, lodging with Barton residents, also sought employment at Hall's Ropery.

Name	Position	Age	Occupation	Place of Birth
William Briggs	Head	79	Road maker	Appleby
John Geffrey	Lodger	29	Roper	Liverpool
1861 Census- St. Mary Parish, Newport Street.				

Many came from the locality (around 60%), but many came from further away, including Liverpool and Scotland. We can only speculate on the circumstances of their eventual move to Barton, and a detailed study of the role of Hull as a 'hub' for immigration could prove an illuminating study for a future historian. It cannot be ruled out that family contacts were important. Similarly, many households took lodgers who, although unrelated, were often born in the same town or village. This could lead us to conjecture that personal networks were instrumental in creating opportunities for several lodgers to follow their friends and families to Barton. Yet the role of the unskilled labourer is rather an enigma in understanding the labour structure of the rope works. Despite possessing the huge benefit of covered workings not subject to the mercy of the weather (thus allowing rope making all year), it is inconceivable that Hall's Ropery would not have benefited from the employment of journeyman labourers, given the seasonal changes in demand for their products (many ships were laid up over winter months throughout the period before steam navigation). Indeed, it is important to think of Hall's labour force not as a fixed population of employees, but rather as a group of workers in constant flux, as few lodgers associated with rope making appear in two consecutive censuses. Ball acknowledges this fact when noting: 'the *average* hands employed at the Ropery is 100'. Study of the 1851 census suggests that the number of permanent workers at Hall's Ropery could even approach half of that figure, perhaps even less would have been regarded as indispensable by Hall's management.

Clearly, the town's population was changing as people moved to find work at the rope works and in other industries. These were manifest in the 1851 census, but had originated in the decades prior to this when we do not have detailed censuses to work from. What had happened in the decades following the formation of works which had created the distinct labour structure visible in the first censuses and Ball's history? It is traditionally argued by historians that enclosure precipitated the birth of a wage economy, and the early history of Hall's Ropery can be used to support this thesis.[12] As we saw in the preceding chapter, parliamentary enclosure enabled the development of land for industry, thus creating the need for labour to fuel increased industrial production.[13] This argument is traditionally associated with the history of agricultural development, but can be justifiably applied to other rural industries, including rope making. The migration of temporary workers, generally living as lodgers, only served to reinforce the wage-earning nature of rope making in Barton. These men lived in Barton purely in the pursuit of wages, a relatively new phenomenon in rural communities, if not in the well developed industrial cities of the North and Midlands.[14] The large number of 'wage migrants' therefore was a significant shift in the way Barton's industry was fed with labour. Following John Hall's development of the rope works on a single site, using increasing capital investment, he helped create the industrial character of the Waterside area.

Whilst some isolated examples of 'home' rope making are recorded in the census, mainly in association with shipbuilding or shop-owning, this was not nearly as important as Hall's industrial concern.

What of the wages at Hall's? The subject is a difficult one for historians to grapple with due to the scarcity of records, inconsistent recording techniques, and the rather different role wages assumed in the nineteenth century economy. Many eminent historians have attempted elaborate reconstructions of English workers' historical wages, with rather mixed success. In Barton, our best attempts suggest that throughout the nineteenth century employment at the rope works was relatively well paid compared to agriculture and other local industry. In the later nineteenth century it was not uncommon for a skilled rope maker to earn between 24 and 27 shillings per week whilst unskilled labourers and minors earned between 5 and 15 shillings.[15] Although direct comparison is difficult, most contemporary sources show agricultural wages, although high in national terms, as somewhere between 17 and 18 shillings per week in Lincolnshire.[16] Contemporary government figures suggest agricultural wages to be around 51-53% of those in industry.[17] It is easy to be blinded by attempting modern reconstructions though; the phrase 'lies, damn lies and statistics' is brought to mind. Unfortunately, without any definitive figures from Barton as an individual town, ideally, from an individual street, where direct comparison would therefore be possible, we must tentatively conclude that ropery workers earned more than most agricultural labourers.

However, paid wages represented only part of an agricultural worker's support network, with valuable allowances often given by farm owners and estate managers. This included assistance with food, housing and even clothing. This method of remuneration for lower wages was something from which the rope makers of Hall's Ropery would not benefit. When these allowances were valued in monetary terms the gap between agricultural labourers and those working in industry was narrowed greatly. So the gap in living standards between agricultural workers and Ropery employees was perhaps not as clear as a simple comparison of wages would suggest.

In a rural society the significance of wages was linked to many other factors. For instance, work in agriculture presented many opportunities to supplement a low income. Times of seeding, harvest, lambing or foaling all provided extra work opportunities for an agricultural labourer. A salaried employee of Hall's would enjoy fewer similar opportunities, but instead probably benefited from more consistent employment. National economic or political factors created and destroyed opportunities for different people at different times, therefore relative incomes could fluctuate wildly during the nineteenth century. For example, during the economic depression of the 1880s, industrial workers' opportunities were curtailed to a much greater extent than in agriculture. It was not until the turn of the twentieth century that the relative advantages agricultural workers enjoyed had disappeared as the cost of living rose.

In conclusion, higher wages did not necessarily guarantee a higher standard of living for Barton's ropers, although at over 24 shillings per week, the highest paid of Hall's employees, the skilled rope makers, were amongst the best paid labourers in Barton's economy. Conversely, the journeyman labourers, those who had no permanent job at the ropery, were perhaps much worse off than those of similar skill levels working in agriculture.

Let us study in detail the instances for which more specific information regarding incomes survives. The *Stamford Mercury* reported a strike at Hall's works in 1853, and we can perhaps interpret this as a culmination of the events of the previous decades. The strike was clearly led by wage earners requesting increased wages rather than improvements to working conditions. The request reported in the *Stamford Mercury* was for an increase in wages of two shillings per week.[18] Low pay had been a pertinent issue at the works for many years, and there is some evidence to suggest a pre-1853 workforce unity over this issue. For instance, in 1852 Matthew Bell, a roper at Hall's, was fined 18 shillings for avoiding a fare on a train between New Holland and Barton. It was his 'companions in the ropery' who decided to pay his fine.[19] We must be careful of placing more significance on this quotation than it can reasonably be expected to bear, but it is possible that pay for some men at the Ropery was recognised as being so poor that the avoidance of a railway fare was effectively condoned (or at least empathised with) by the workforce as a whole. This small flash of information is perhaps one of the few contextual sources we have to ascertain the unity and beliefs of Hall's employees.

Rex Russell, a Barton historian, interpreted the strike as a first exercise of the newly defined (and newly vocal) wage-earning class, specifically in association with the newly formed (1851) *Working Man's Association*.[20] As we demonstrated above, the development of the works had seen the factory system triumph in the years before 1851. However, the degree to which outside Associations were involved in any agitation by Barton's workforce is an area of the town's history that requires a much more focused study in the future. To pursue Russell's interpretation though, we can surmise that the permanent, skilled, rope makers of Barton were instrumental in securing the prosperity of Hall's works, and it is therefore plausible that they were aware of the 'leverage' they held over the company. Further study of this interesting issue, using Russell's work as a starting point, could prove very interesting. The pay claim was eventually settled in October of that year when a compromise was reached.

Importantly though, the strike represented the beginnings of clearer perceptions in Barton of a Waterside community, perhaps even a Waterside 'class'. The very act of submitting a report of the strike to the *Stamford Mercury* is significant as it was rare for contributors to the newspaper to mention industrial issues. Its inclusion therefore betrays a fundamental contemporary distinction between capital and labour an- 'us and them' mentality, as it were. It appears that John Hall and his family recognised, and perhaps chimed with this polarised view of 'master and worker', as they set up a works brass band in 1859, and followed that by the construction of a mission chapel in 1864.[21] Both of these actions were conspicuously lauded by Barton's elite, whose voice was once again, found in the *Stamford Mercury*. It seems that John Hall, and his son John Edward, limited their engagement in the town to these few acts of what could be called philanthropy (using a modern understanding of the term), thereby showing little interest in upsetting the hegemony of Barton's traditional clerical and professional ruling elite in matters of local politics. John Hall remained a member of the *Old Friendly Society,* but with membership declining it is unlikely that this society was very active by 1851.[22] Yet the construction of a mission chapel as an integral part of the works buildings was a powerful statement; literally bringing the local populace to the works, it must have served to create strong cultural links between rope works, town, and within the Waterside community itself. John Hall did engage in social philanthropy in his home community of Hull, subscribing to reading rooms, schools, and even the *Botanic Society,* as well as his well recorded involvement with Hull's Maritime establishment at *Trinity House*.[23] These activities illustrate an interesting contrast between his interests in Barton and Hull, leading us to conclude that John Hall's philanthropic endeavours in Barton were very closely focused on his rope works and those who were in his employ.

At John Edward Hall's personal expense, a Mission Chapel was constructed as part of the works in 1864. Subsequently converted to storage space it is photographed here before its demolition in 1990.

photo - courtesy Brian Peeps

John Hall aged 88 years.

John's son, John Edward Hall, was perhaps more interested in the material predicament of his workforce. Rev. Charles Moor, Vicar of Barton, kept detailed notes on the very poorest of Barton's inhabitants, and speculated that one old roper was 'helped' by the Halls. Similarly John Edward's personal gardener, Martin Toogood, also served as caretaker for the Mission Room and worked for Hall into his seventies.[24] His son George worked in the rope works, although their poverty was enough for them to be mentioned in Moor's notebooks. Such a work arrangement could be interpreted as having paternalist connotations. On the whole though, Moor's notebooks show that few ropers required charitable assistance, implying that their employment was relatively well paid and stable. Those that were mentioned were usually referred to as the 'deserving' poor, a Victorian term used to describe those finding themselves in poverty through illness, injury and other 'misfortune', rather than the perceived evils of drink and indolence. We can therefore suggest that the ropers' respectability in the eyes of elites such as Moor was high. Perhaps John Edward shared these views when he was prepared to help his poorer employees.

As Hall's rope works became established, it is evident that the tradition of seeking employment there was passed from generation to generation. For instance, the 1861 census shows James Daddy was born in Barton around 1809 and his brother Edward in 1812. By 1861 both found themselves labouring at the rope works. Successive generations of the family worked as rope makers, living in three separate households by the turn of the twentieth century.[25] Such trends were not rare in nineteenth century industry as a whole, but it is important to note that rope making conformed to this.

Children often followed their parents into work at the Ropery, and stayed into their adult working life. All of the rope makers in the Daddy family had become associated with the trade before they were of adult age. Indeed, the familial nature of working at the Ropery is a distinct feature of labour structure in the nineteenth century. Other than journeyman workers, there were few families associated with rope making which had only one member in the employ of the firm, and in many cases both the head of the family, his wife and all their children were occupied in the various parts of the rope making process. The 'family element', as it may be described in the language of today, was shared with the brick and tile industry, and was a major contributory factor to the character of the Waterside community. This emphasis on children working at the rope works was noted by contemporary school masters, who in 1878 wrote:

> 'Many are at work that ought to be at school - brickmakers and ropemakers seem to care nothing for the regulations.'[26]

It is interesting that this criticism is very different from many rural communities where poor attendance was usually associated with the needs of the agricultural community. The disruption to education in this case was often sporadic, whereas employment at the rope works in Barton represented a deliberate and irreversible alternative to formal education. The well recorded propensity for parents to send their children to work at the works helped reinforce the distinct social colouring of the Waterside area, especially in regard to the reported success of Sunday schooling, something which could be pursued whilst still following full time employment during the week.

Steam powered machinery to spin yarns had been introduced in Barton by 1851, and had made the overall process of rope making much more efficient.[27] The history of hemp-spinning is an interesting one in itself. Firstly, it is apparent that spinning of hemp by machine was quickly seized upon as a suitable task for female workers. Importantly, this represented a shift from the home to the factory, as spinning had usually been carried on at the former.[28] Female labour appears to have been permanent in nature, with most employed women appearing in successive censuses because the company was keen, having invested heavily in steam-powered spinning machinery, to keep this process efficient, centralised, and therefore reliable. The role of female labour will be studied in greater detail in a later chapter.

Historical accounts of other rope manufacturers, record that hand spinning survived for many decades after the introduction of machine spinning, so the true number of hand spinners in nineteenth century Barton is impossible to quantify from rather poorly enumerated census data.[29] However, there is no evidence of any reluctance by Hall's to adopt machine spinning, as no record is made of any tension between hand spinners and management which occurred in many other works. These disputes have often been interpreted as the main factor in the survival of hand-spinning throughout the later part of the nineteenth century. Census Returns show that the occupation of 'spinner' became less common as a discernable occupation as the century progressed. It seems that the 'bringing in' of spinning to complete the whole process of rope making at Hall's site was one of the final acts in the creation of a complete factory system and therefore an 'industrial' Barton. To illustrate the foresight of John Hall, it must be noted that as early as 1832, along with Mr. Hassell and Mr. Todd, he endeavoured to set up the *Hull Flax and Cotton Mill*.[30] A speculative enterprise to exploit the booming trade in cotton and linen, it nevertheless illustrates John Hall's determination to create a complete industrial portfolio, which encompassed all parts of the rope and sailcloth making process from supply (which he negotiated with various hemp traders, including relatives based in South Shields), processing and finally, rope making itself. It is not too large a leap of faith to suggest that Hall's involvement with the Hull Mill in the early 1830s directly led to his setting up of machine spinning at Barton.

Spinning twine by hand was a skilled occupation, and survived beyond the introduction of steam-powered machinery. Here one spinner is shown operating the simple mechanism, but hooks were provided for up to eight men to work at once. 'Turning the wheel' was a laborious job, and was usually performed by children.

Importantly, the lack of recorded tension between capital and labour, in regard to the introduction of machine spinning, suggests a labour force unable to actively negotiate their status. In the textile industry, the artisan status of workers meant a very vibrant discourse between employers and employees was possible.[31] In cases recorded at some rope manufacturers, 'masters and journeymen' objected to the introduction of machinery in a similar fashion. Journeymen presumably lost out to machinery as it provided Hall's with a constant and reliable supply of material using a permanent, and crucially, a small workforce. Opportunities for piecework were effectively removed. Some of these disputes were formalised through trade associations, such as that in Liverpool in 1821, and Birmingham in 1868, but generally the stage for these disputes was individual rope manufacturers.[32] The general historical interpretation is that these disputes failed, and where 'artisan' sentiments remained, companies would ultimately fail as well through an inability to compete effectively with rope manufacturers operating a factory system.

By the 1870s Hall's Ropery was a significant rope manufacturer, but one that was unusual in its location in a small town. Rope works which had survived industrialisation, and indeed grown because of it, such as *Gourock Rope Works* (Glasgow), were located in heavily populated areas and hence had access to a substantial indigenous labour supply. There is considerable evidence that Hall's rope works continued to attract migrant labour throughout the nineteenth century, with the strong family element in its labour structure serving to retain those families in the long-term.[33] This is in direct contrast to the relative decline in agricultural labour Barton experienced.[34] This curious balance of labour migration is perhaps rare in the demographics of rural towns in Lincolnshire as the predominantly industrial centres of Gainsborough, Grantham and Boston were arguably no longer 'rural' towns by the 1870s; having little or no interest in agricultural *production*.[35] The growing importance of the company within Barton can be gauged from records which show Hall's owning cottages on Ings Road from 1884, a brickyard occupied by J.W. Briggs from 1887, and from 1888, agricultural land rented to local farmers.[36] In 1890, Hall's Ropery was re-formed as a private limited company. The company's role in creating an industrial Barton was emphasised in its new name, Hall's Barton Ropery Co. Ltd.

3. Women's work

There must always be a proportion of men on the engineering and maintenance sides, in supervisory grades, and for hard and skilled labour in the ropewalks, but the spinning frames need the nimble-fingered, patient girls to serve them. It applies equally in this trade as in the cotton towns of Lancashire; so that for more than a century the female operative has been key to labour in the ropery.

W. Tyson, *Rope. A History*, 1966. [1]

And so, it would appear, we could leave it at that! Tyson certainly felt so. His survey of the rope industry, although written in 1966, was seemingly representative of attitudes a century earlier. At the very least, the quotation invites us to study the interpretation suggested by Tyson, and therefore aspire to bring a critical approach to attitudes to the role of women in the rope works. It may also prove useful to study further Tyson's suggestion that female labour in the rope industry was directly comparable to that in the cotton industry.

Of course, women had always been involved in rope making; at the very time John Hall inherited his father's rope making business in 1802 various sources record that women who spun flax and hemp could expect to make 3s. a day for their labours.[2] Arthur Young, in his survey of Britain written during the eighteenth century, noted that women were heavily engaged in the growing and processing of hemp and flax. In Shropshire, a seminal study of rural economies revealed a subsistence hemp cultivation system whereby cottage dwellers rented between ten and fifteen perches of land (about half the size of a modern tennis court.) at eighteen shillings a year and combined this with the industry of the household's female labour to make enough money to pay for the annual rent of the entire property. Indeed, this profit which was made by women spinning the home-grown hemp could often approach four pounds a year, a not insignificant sum given the small scale of the cultivation.[3] Some evidence of this hemp growing can be identified in modern villages, the name 'Hempland' a common remnant of this once important crop.

When the first rope making factory was established in Barton, female labour was instrumental in the process of rope making. The new factory relied upon hand-spun yarns, and thus home-spinning carried on as it had done for centuries, relying on women to provide the labour. However, imported hemp was used at the Barton factory early in its existence and the cultivation of local hemp quickly became unprofitable.[4] Spinning on 'piece-work' rates became the norm, women receiving pay directly from Hall's for their *labour* rather than their products, the hemp itself remaining the property of Hall's Ropery throughout the transaction. This chimes well with current academic research which has sought to demonstrate that the role of female labourers was not a choice of 'work place or home', where the two were mutually exclusive; but one of 'work place *and* home'.[5]

Yet, as rope making became more technologically distinct from other crafts such as sail cloth manufacture, it appears that a hierarchy of roles developed. At the rope works in Chatham (Kent), the spinners were men because their skilled labour was needed to provide yarns of suitable lengths for the very largest ships. They were specialist spinners, exclusively involved in the rope making industry. Female labourers were most likely engaged in the spinning of smaller twines and yarns for sailcloth weaving. There was a place for women in Hall's Ropery, but it appears it was becoming increasingly marginalised as Hall's emphasis turned from small twines and sailcloth, to larger ropes.

Steam-powered machinery began to be used in the preparation of hemp and flax from the 1840s.

When, by 1861, the first female spinners were recorded as working within Hall's factory, it could be interpreted as the natural culmination of the industrial system John Hall had been developing since the early 1800s. Fundamentally, the introduction of female labour at Barton corresponded with the mechanisation of the spinning process.[6] Whilst the *role* of spinning hemp could, in part, still be attributed to women, the *means* was, by around 1850, firmly invested in the factory and its machinery. It would appear that whatever John Hall's personal views of women in factories were, their employment for spinning hemp was potentially a less contentious issue because it did not introduce female labour to traditionally male roles. Tyson argued that the impact of machine spinning was actually rather limited; male hand spinning still remained a part of the rope making industry until the 1890s, with superior quality and flexibility of specification being cited as the main reasons for maintaining this method. It is therefore plausible that in Barton, the hierarchy of male and female spinning roles continued after the introduction of machine spinning. Male hand spinners were not directly threatened by the introduction of female workers, as traditional gendered roles were still strictly reinforced. In fact, machine spinning probably served to emphasise the difference in skill between male and female labour. This theory fits nicely with the general acceptance of female labour in the Victorian cotton and textile industry, where women entered factories to pursue traditionally female roles of spinning and weaving, whilst reinforcing the 'superiority' of male labour.[7]

The 'Victorian domestic ideology', allegedly attacked female workers because of their *place* of work, stating, at its most simple, that women simply did not belong in factories.[8] However, it becomes clear from study of the women in Barton rope works, coupled with the experience of the cotton industry, that the pertinent issue in Victorian ideology was the *role* of women, not necessarily their place of work. When Victorian workplace legislation is considered, it shows us that governments rarely banned female labour from specific places of work. When such bans were put in place; for example the 1842 Mines Act (banning women from working underground), the place of work was merely an indicator of the unsuitability of the actual role the women fulfilled there, due to its encroachment on male roles.[9] Similar legislation did not exist for other industries and it seems female work, even in Britain's factories, was not wrong, *per se,* as long as it chimed with the Victorian ideology of recognised female roles. Hall's Ropery, with its large number of female employees, was a very good example of this ideology 'in action'.

So what was the women's role at the rope works? In terms of finished products little had changed with the coming of mechanisation. It was consistently the job of women to ensure the Ropery received a constant supply of spun flax and hemp, an 1842 report of a Leeds Flax Mill stated quite clearly that 'the workpeople employed being almost exclusively females'.[10] Barton's flax and hemp mills were probably employing most of the spinners in Barton by the 1850s, with few remaining at home.[11] In many ways the mechanised process of spinning hemp and flax was comparable to the tasks women performed in the Lancashire cotton industry, but many contemporary observers noted the increased labour involved in preparing hemp and flax compared to the 'finer' art of cotton spinning. In 1842, around 18 women were employed on one 'bank' of flax and hemp spinning machines, transferring the materials between hackling machines, collecting tow, and finally running the spinning machines.[12] The spinning itself was often done when the fibres (especially finer flax, which was used for weaving sailcloth) were soaked in warm water. This was done by introducing steam to a trough of water to warm it, then soaking the flax in this. As the flax was spun at more than 1000 revolutions per minute it is reported that water 'was thrown off at a continuous force', requiring the women attending the machine to wear waterproofed aprons.[13] The results, in the words of mill owners, was a team of mill workers producing 'around one-hundred times more spun yarn each day' than could be achieved using a 'domestic system of piece-work'.[14]

Female labour was almost exclusively used in the mechanised preparation of hemp and flax, and Hall's had a significant number of female factory operatives by 1861.

Victorians saw the whole process of spinning hemp and flax as 'rougher' than that of cotton, silk or even wool. This is interesting in itself. The handling of flax and hemp fibres did require more physical effort than in the cotton industry, but this was probably due in greater part to the differing levels of capital investment in machinery than actual toil inherent to the processing of each type of fibre. Flax and hemp, unlike cotton, wool and silk, were low value materials, and with a few exceptions (notably Huddart & Co in London, Gourock near Glasgow, and Chatham and Portsmouth Naval rope works), spinning was done on a much smaller scale than the in cotton industry.[15] For example by the mid nineteenth century 380,000 workers were employed in cotton spinning, but only 7% of that figure in the whole rope industry.[16] It is a natural assumption that capital investment was lower in hemp spinning than in the highly mechanised cotton and textiles industries. With lower levels of mechanisation more physical effort was required when spinning hemp and flax, and it is interesting that in Victorian commentary the end product itself was regarded as 'rough'.[17] Sailcloth, and other flax-based textiles were cheap, poorly graded materials, and like hemp was merely part of a wider industrial process; together they were both utilitarian, industrial products. It appears from contemporary comment that the status of those who worked these materials was accordingly low: a rough cloth, produced with rough hands. The labour required was therefore perceived as relatively unskilled, and by following Victorian logic to its conclusion, suitable for women.

Still, mechanisation promised higher capacity for Hall's Ropery. The mechanisation of spinning clearly reinforced the existing hierarchy of male-female labour. Roles occupied by men were never penetrated by women workers, the reasons given for this usually being the superior strength and experience of the male labourer.[18] This of course was reflected in wages, with female workers usually expected to earn around 60% of a male unskilled-labourer's wage, and perhaps as little as 30% of a male worker with a comparable skill level.[19] In the cotton industry it appears that many women breached these employment barriers to become supervisors or 'skilled' workers, but in the 'rough' flax and hemp spinning industry no such opportunities existed; rope makers were men, spinners were women. Most contemporary engravings emphasise this dichotomy.

Differing roles.
To the left a woman is pictured 'drawing the fibre', which after spinning into yarn was formed into rope by the men on the ropewalk (right). These strictly gendered roles were never interchangeable.

Perhaps the simplest way to think of the role of female labour is in terms of skill. Until recently it was accepted that 'going to the factories' led to a 'de-skilling' of Britain's Victorian workforce. This was not so; the dexterity and patience required from female workers, alluded to in our opening quotation, required a high level of skill, despite an attitude that the tasks performed were somehow inferior to those of men. This institutionalised attitude to 'skill' remained in the division of work at the rope works (in at least some recognisable form) throughout the nineteenth and twentieth century, and arguably until the closure of the works itself in the 1980s.

Who, then, were the female Ropery labourers? In line with the textile industry, and domestic service, it appears Ropery work fitted the national and local trends for young women workers who were generally aged between 14 and 25, unmarried, and members of families associated with the same occupation. A brief, and cautious, look at the female population structure using Census Returns, suggest around 65-75% of all female Ropery workers were aged below 25. Of these, the overwhelming majority (80%) were unmarried or widowed. In terms of the Victorian 'domestic ideology' this makes perfect sense. In 1833 a factory inspector in Lancashire wrote that young girls were desirable workers as their strength was no less than boys of the same age and 'they are more docile and obedient'.[20] Women above this age, i.e. married, were perhaps not suitable due to their perceived primary role as home-makers and mothers.

In 1894 a Government report gave the primary reason for women working as 'death of the head of the family'.[21] This can certainly be identified in Barton's censuses, as many entries showed widows, often together with their daughters, working in the rope works as spinners. Whereas the average age for spinners was around 20 years old, widows as old as 60 are recorded as continuing to spin in an attempt to provide a sufficient family wage.

The rope works also seems to have been the haven for the dispossessed and desperate. For instance, unmarried female lodgers, unaccompanied by any relatives, form a considerable part of the workforce. Whilst this was common, indeed necessary for 'live-in' domestic service, such economic migrants were relatively rare in other areas of Victorian society. This suggests a certain level of desperation. Similarly, widowed women who took in lodgers were usually of undoubted poverty:

Name	Position in Family	Age	Occupation	Where Born
Elizabeth Pirle	Head	38	In receipt of Relief	Barton
Thomas Tack	Lodger	62	Hemp Weaver	Winterton

Whilst this example illustrates the poverty behind these arrangements it should not be taken as representative; generally female lodgers stayed with female landladies, who were usually spinners themselves (unless too old to be working or in receipt of poor-relief).

Whilst migrant female workers were an interesting element of the work force; their significance must not be over stated. The majority of female Ropery workers were born in

Barton, to parents who were associated with rope making and usually lived in the Waterside area. Let us take one illustrative example of a Barton roper's family recorded in 1861:

Name	Position in Family	Age	Occupation	Where Born
Thomas Newton	Head	40	Rope maker	Stoke Bridge, Lancs.
Mary	Wife	36		Barton
Mary	Daughter	17	Hemp spinner	Barton
Ellen	Daughter	15	'Hemp'	Barton
Margaret	Daughter	12	'Hemp'	Barton

In this case it is clear that with three female members of the family working for wages, even if only five shillings a week, their role in the family economy was important.[22] This was common in many Barton households involved in rope making, and goes some way to demonstrating the importance of understanding female labour in the context of a family income.

Female labour, confined to spinning in the earlier years of mechanisation, began to branch into other jobs within the rope industry as mechanisation removed traditional skills and physical effort from rope making. Developments in rope making machinery moved fast in the later nineteenth century: three-strand laying machines were introduced in the 1880s, cabling machines around 1890 and horizontal stranding machines not much later.[23] These innovations chiefly concerned themselves with the speeding up and simplification of manufacturing processes, and subsequently saw women labourers employed in the rope mills as well as the spinning sheds. The parallels with women's jobs in the cotton industry became much clearer. From around the mid 1880s the increase in female labour became noticeable, and relentless. At Barton, verifiable census figures suggest around 33% of the workforce was female. The figures for the nation as a whole were recorded in detail, and in 1891 (in the whole industry) there were 100 women employed for every 350 men. By 1911 only 150 men were employed for the same number of women.[24]

Women's roles in the rope making industry remained similar throughout the late nineteenth and early twentieth century. The gradual increase in the number of women employed continued until the late 1930s when female labour finally outnumbered the men employed in the industry.[25] Wages throughout the early twentieth century remained low and shifts were long, but work at the Ropery represented an important opportunity to add to the family income.

Women's Work

Broadly speaking the female workforce employed at the Ropery in the late 1930s was similar in make-up to that in the nineteenth century, the women being young, unmarried and remaining at the works only as long as this situation prevailed. This continuity, in part derived from managerial attitudes. Some former employees recall that the works manager A. Hendy held strictly traditional views of women's work. Subsequently, married women were rarely employed.

Women changing the bobbins on the company's hemp spinning machines.

photo - courtesy David Lee

The most momentous change of the twentieth century was brought by the coming of the Second World War. Whilst the nature of employment for women did not strictly change much, the context of wartime lent it a new significance. As an important industry for the war effort, it was necessary to maintain staff levels as production soared. Longer shifts, often lasting throughout the night, ensured women workers were much more engaged in labouring at the rope works than before. Part of this engagement included the employment of married women. Although skilled male ropers, who worked on the ropewalk, were classed as being in a reserved occupation and so exempt from military service, general male labourers were not. As the greater part of the male workforce was conscripted, the works relied increasingly on female labour, very much in the same way thousands of women worked in Britain's munitions and engineering factories.[26] In the post-war period, unlike experience elsewhere where men returned to resume their positions and displaced women workers, the rope industry maintained its reliance on female labour. Indeed, males never again outnumbered females in the country's rope works. Similarly, as synthetic fibres and materials were developed in the post-war period, it is argued by historians that male labour relegated women to lesser roles, the fetching and carrying as it were.[27] The introduction of synthetic fibre for weaving changed women's roles in the rayon industry but this was not so in Hall's Barton Ropery. When synthetic fibres were introduced women continued in broadly similar roles as before. One possible reason for this was that synthetic fibre rope making methods had much in common with natural fibre rope making.[28] Therefore handling of synthetic fibres was limited to forming ropes, and remained little different from the processes in which Hall's female workers had become skilled.

Whilst many women employees of Hall's Barton Ropery saw the work as temporary, in the post-war period many women stayed at the works on a long-term basis, rising to positions of responsibility. Some women worked at the rope works for more than 40 years, adding much to the maternal element of the way the shop-floor was organised. Until the advent of health and safety policy in the later 1970s, much of the day to day safety and general running of the mills was left to the discretion of these more senior female employees, lending the rope mills a distinct working atmosphere, perhaps unique in Barton's industrial heritage.

Madge Audsley joined Hall's Barton Ropery in 1936 at the age of 14, staying with the company for 46 years.

photo - Brian Peeps

4. Rope For War

Hall's Barton Ropery had a long association with wartime work and the firm's involvement in Britain's wartime production is well recorded, not least by those who once worked there. This chapter will look beyond wartime events at Hall's Ropery, to see how international events impacted on the company's suppliers, markets, and employees.

An early business card for John Hall's ropery, proudly displaying the company's Admiralty patronage, something which the company profited greatly throughout its long history.

The story of wartime work in Hall's Ropery begins with the personal story of John Hall. By using contacts he had gained through his association with Hull Trinity House, he ensured that the Admiralty utilised his Ropery to produce 'massive government stores' during the Napoleonic War.[1] It is probable that he profited considerably from this. Indeed during the first decade of the nineteenth century, dominated as it was by the conflict, Admiralty orders probably contributed greatly to Hall's ability to finance permanent and substantial buildings in Barton. However, it is likely that the greatest part of his wealth came from personal, speculative enterprises. On the most basic level his civilian shipping activity became very profitable, as the heightened risks of wartime shipping were rewarded financially. Still, one detailed study of shipping risks during the Napoleonic War suggests bulk cargoes such as hemp were possibly less affected. On the whole, privateering was a 'bloodless' aspect of the war and ships laden with hemp were not the glittering prizes the French privateers sought. Indeed, in 1799, the ships *Rover* and *Guilford,* bound from Koningsberg to Grimsby, were both captured, but only their valuable goods were seized; the ships' hemp cargo was left untouched and the ships made it to Grimsby.[2] So, whilst the actual loss of bulk cargoes like hemp was low, the perceived threat to shipping (becoming almost hysteria during 1799-1805) led to the introduction of a convoy system for all shipping.[3] Ships could only be insured if running as part of these large convoys which only sailed every few months, and this disrupted trade in Hull. More frequent sailings were possible only by doing so without insurance. This was probably less of a risk for Hall who was shipping bulk goods, enabling him to exploit and profit from the prevailing trading situation. Clearly, a trader willing to run his ship without insurance (which ran at around 12% in 1806) had a significant advantage in Hull's hungry market place.[4]

Further to this, the privateering contracts we know John Hall engaged in could reap financial rewards of many thousands of pounds. Merely leasing his ship *Aurora* for troop transport duties returned several hundred pounds.[5] It appears that John Hall was a 'war opportunist.' Even in his later years he ensured his ships engaged in the very profitable trade with the rebel Confederate States during the American Civil War. Records show that one of his ships, the *Ruby*, was running armaments during this conflict, so these activities clearly did not directly involve the interests of his Ropery.[6] Such ventures were not always profitable however, as records survive which show he lost one ship to the French in 1815, and the *Ruby* itself to the Federal States of the USA in 1863.[7] Rather than directly profiteering from war production, John Hall tended to profit from the economic and mercantile effects of war. The mid-nineteenth century Crimean War was a case in point. By 1850, British industry had come to rely on the supply of Russian hemp, importing, on average around 15,000 tons per annum at a value of around £600,000.[8] When this supply was closed as Britain entered a state of war with Russia, John Hall immediately re-established the cultivation of hemp in Barton to secure a reliable and cheap supply.[9]

These spurious ship's papers were kept by the company as a memento of the failed gun-running trip John Hall's ship *Ruby*, attempted in 1863. A Federal Eagle was engraved on the reverse of a tobacco manufacturer's brass plaque.

Much of the preceding discourse is the story of the wartime enterprises of John Hall himself, and not the Ropery *as a company*; it seems there was little sense of duty or patriotism in John Hall's dealing with wartime conditions. It may be that William Ball, writing about the ropeworks in 1852 applies a patriotic tone to the company's Napoleonic War effort, but it seems clear from John Hall's actions that private speculation was the order of the day. That is not to say that John Hall's role in the Napoleonic War was unimportant; quite the contrary. The role of the privateer or wartime speculator is currently under-researched by historians, and undoubtedly their role has been minimised in a period of history dominated until very recently by the grand discourses of Trafalgar, Austerlitz and Waterloo.[10]

In a similar way that the Crimean War had affected the supplies of Russian hemp, the 1898 Spanish American War impacted on the embryonic trade in manila. The United States of America imposed a 30 shillings per ton duty on manila exported from their recently occupied Philippine Islands, and thus almost immediately removed around 50% of the London market in favour of American traders.[11] The manila hemp which did make it to Britain was no longer controlled by the London dealers, making speculation in raw manila a profitable diversion for even the smallest of rope manufacturers. It is inconceivable that Hall's Ropery did not engage in this activity to some extent, especially when many smaller rope manufacturers (in the Barton and Grimsby area) required local suppliers of hemp.

The intricacies of raw material supply are often shaped by conflict, perhaps no more so than during the two World Wars of the twentieth-century. The arms race of the early twentieth century, culminating in the Great War of 1914-1918 is well documented. It is likely that Hall's Barton Ropery benefited financially from this 'race', focussing as it did on Admiralty contracts. As early as 1908, Hall's Barton Ropery had produced ropes suitable to tow a Dreadnought Battleship, then the last word in technological achievement.[12] Great prestige and pride were attached to fulfilling these orders, and the company maintained a strong nationalist rhetoric throughout the early twentieth century.[13] Their links with the Admiralty served the company well, placing it in the vanguard of rope production when conflict finally, and inevitably, broke out in 1914. Some references to Hall's Barton Ropery survive in Naval logbooks in the National Archives, Kew.[14] It is likely that many more are deeply buried in Admiralty records. The company's involvement in the arms race was not exclusively related to British naval contracts, as Japan's naval build-up resulted in rope orders throughout the first two decades of the twentieth century.[15] This was probably robustly supported by the British Government, who endeavoured to make trading conditions favourable for the Japanese Navy to acquire a complete, technologically advanced fleet, constructed and fitted out almost solely in British shipyards.

The 1914-1918 war posed several problems with the supply of hemp. With German control of the Baltic, supply chains were severed or carried on under the constant threat of ships being lost to enemy action. Prices of hemp therefore rose sharply in the early part of the war, due to the increased difficulty in successfully importing the material.[16] After three years of successively tighter trade restrictions the War Department took direct control of hemp and flax supplies in 1917.[17] Companies such as Hall's Barton Ropery would have little difficulty in obtaining hemp to fulfil military orders, due to their record of supplying the Admiralty in the preceding decade. Employment was, therefore, constant and stable throughout the war, unaffected as it was by conscription when it was introduced in 1916. Smaller rope manufacturers fared less well, and with their capacity not being great enough to provide a meaningful contribution to war supplies, they found themselves seriously struggling to obtain any of the limited supplies of raw material.[18] Hall's Barton Ropery's private business came close to a complete halt as the war progressed for, as part of government control of the industry in 1917, licences were required for export. These were often not forthcoming for products that were needed more urgently for the British war effort.

East African sisal plantations were developed in earnest after the First World War, and much of the local labour economy was focussed on them. This picture dates from the 1950s.

The Great War also interrupted raw material supplies as they rapidly became valuable strategic assets for the conflicting nations. For instance, in the immediate pre-war period East African sisal plantations had been established. However, the war disrupted production in these German colonies. Indeed, the great colonial campaigns in Africa are some of the most forgotten of the war, and the securing of sisal plantations was a significant factor in the motives behind this conflict which limited the use of sisal during wartime. The industry was only in its embryonic stages, however, and after the war the British mandate in these colonies ensured it was British industry which benefited from the re-establishment and development of the plantations. Lord

Milner, the Colonial Secretary in the 1920s, emphasised the need to build up production in these colonies - modern day Rwanda and Burundi.[19]

The end of the Great War in 1918 did not immediately relieve problems of supply. In 1919, the supply of Russian hemp, which was problematic during the conflict, turned to catastrophe. The Russian Revolution turned to civil war, Britain supported Czarist sympathisers and accordingly the Soviet Government deliberately paralysed British trade; an act that reverberated throughout British manufacturing industry. The crisis was felt keenly by rope manufacturers who relied upon Russia for their supply of raw materials. Furthermore, with its traditionally strong Baltic links, the port of Hull was badly affected. Subsequently, supplies of fibre were sourced in Italy, continuing a trend that had developed during the Great War.[20] Hall's Barton Ropery secured an agent in Genoa, as most rope manufacturers had done during the 1920s.

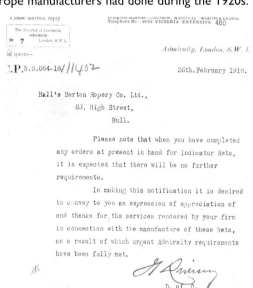

A letter from the Admiralty, 1918.

How did Hall's Barton Ropery turn the wartime conditions and post-war recovery to its advantage? The language of nationalism and patriotism pervaded the company's attitude much more than in the previous century. Aspects of 'duty' were very much emphasised in the company's literature. Indeed the company's 1924 publication elevated a rather ordinary letter of confirmation from the Admiralty to pride of place in the promotional book.[21] The language used by the company goes further than a simple emphasis of their role in the supply of materials during the recent war, describing instead how the company directed its energies to '*combating* the submarine campaign' (my italics).[22] Such emotive language shows how Hall's used the conflict, as most manufacturers did, as an essential advertising device during the 1920s. Their role was described as an active one; something which perhaps the rope workers themselves may have struggled to understand so far from the battlefields.

In a period in which nationalistic sentiment was common, good wartime credentials simply meant good business. Hall's Barton Ropery was more discreet in their use of these credentials than many other companies, especially the emergent automobile and civil aviation industries who ran proud, if rather tenuous, advertisements proclaiming they were offering to the public the very same product which had 'won the war'. Alas, there are no longer members of Barton's community who remember the role of the Ropery in the years of the Great War, but as we shall see, the way Hall's Barton Ropery engaged in the language of patriotism and duty was repeated, by company and workers alike in the Second World War. Still, the company's role in wartime production plays an important part in understanding the history of the Ropery in the community. We have seen in previous chapters how there are few instances of the rope works engaging directly in the community of Barton; how John Hall was not of the tradition of great social philanthropists.[23] Yet during the Great War it seems that the rope works was placed at the centre of Barton's own conception of its involvement in the war.

Hall's was keen to protect its independence, and produced this anti-Trade Association literature. They believed such price fixing schemes were of disadvantage to both their customers and the industry generally.

In 1918, once the smoke had settled in Europe, the economic and political situation was irretrievably different from that of 1914. The crisis in Russian hemp supplies and the general over-production of rope factories still geared for war work caused very real concerns in Barton and for the industry as a whole.[24] In politics, a new era of regulation and control began to protect the industry, and help overcome the legacy of wartime. In 1920 the *British Hemp Rope Manufacturers Association* was formed to 'protect and foster the general interests of the hemp rope making industry'.[25] Hall's Barton Ropery was a member, but the Association was plagued with problems as it tried to fix price structures in a volatile economic environment. A major problem was the relative animosity between Britain's rope manufacturers. In this period 'work's pride' was bound very much to company independence. Like any other rope manufacturer, Hall's was keen to uphold its independence once it was threatened by increasingly centralised control of the industry, and the increasing trading power of larger companies such as *British Ropes*.[26] It was about this time that company literature began to publicise the long history of the company, and new emphasis was placed on the 'Hallmark' as a brand. Associations which aimed to negotiate trade arrangements and tariffs with the Government were also formed. Overproduction was a major problem in the industry and, as a result, problems with worker relations, supply and sales were often magnified.

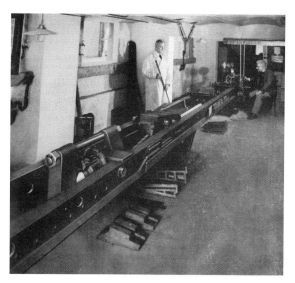

Rope testing apparatus was installed in both the Barton and Beverley works during the 1930s. Measurable quality was an important sales tool.

A further effect of the Great War and associated 'war-work' was the acceleration of centralised standards for products. The *British Engineering Standards Institution* was formed in 1901, with specific reference to steel and engineering. Until the Great War it had remained focused on what could be described as the 'core' products of Britain: steel girders, rail, ship plating and so forth.[27] However, the needs of wartime saw an explosion in the use of standards, reaching rope manufacture for such important products as towing hawsers, and ship's lifeboat ropes; where failure could be catastrophic.[28] By 1930, standards for even the smallest of yarns were in place. Hall's reacted to this trend by investing heavily in testing and measurement machinery, replacing what had previously been done by outside testing companies sanctioned by the Board of Trade.[29] Crucially, the propensity for orders of ropes that needed to reach various British standards served to secure the company's business, whereas for many smaller rope manufacturers who could not meet such standards, it completed the process of destruction that wartime supply problems had begun. Throughout the 1920s the ability to produce strong rope could be quantified much better than in previous years, and Hall's Barton Ropery, like all rope manufacturers, was keen to publicise their ability to produce *measurable* quality. This reinforced the conscious effort by the company to bolster the reputation of their brand-name, 'Hallmark'.

First appearing in the 1920s, 'Hallmark' ropes became a notable brand name in shipping and industry throughout the world.

The term 'inter-war years' is one only used with hindsight. For Hall's Barton Ropery the 1920s were definite 'post-war' years as they re-aligned the company to succeed in a world after the 'war to end all wars'; a world where military orders fell-off abruptly and dramatically. When Arthur Barton Hall succeeded Thomas H. Sissons as Chairman in 1920, the company was in a strong position to adapt to this new economic situation, expanding enough during wartime to successfully invest in the pursuit of new markets. This proved to be the company's salvation for, after eighteen months of relative prosperity, Britain's economy collapsed and hopes of returning to a stable pre-war economy were shattered. The British government's attempts to re-enter the Gold Standard by 1925 also curtailed many export opportunities.

Arthur Barton Hall (1865-1951) became Chairman of the company in 1920.

Hall's Barton Ropery, almost certainly survived because of the new pre-eminence of their wire rope subsidiary company, Overton Brothers. Whilst demand for natural ropes remained high, wartime conditions meant wire rope was used not only in greater quantities for traditional uses such as shipping, but also for new uses including submarine nets, aircraft guy wires (the relatively recent invention of the aeroplane was still a fragile enough contraption to require strong wire bracing), haulage, and even finding its place in the trenches of the Western Front.[30] In the inter-war period many of these uses translated well to civilian markets, especially burgeoning civil aviation and more established haulage and lifting applications. It was at this time Hall's established new markets in Poland and Argentina, with a special focus on the oil and mining industries being developed there.[31] The wire rope division was the salvation of the Barton site, absorbing their losses to the extent of over £10,000 in some years.[32] Many wire ropes required natural fibre cores, which also provided the Barton site with employment.[33] In the later 1920s it appears that consistently more was spent on developing the site at Beverley than in Barton. The result of this development meant that by 1939 wire rope production had quadrupled from that of 1936.[34] Accordingly profit of the whole company rose steadily in the later 1930s, from £4320 in 1934 to over £10,000 by 1939 thus reflecting the company's increase in capital investment from £52,000 to over £70,000 over the same period.[35] Much of this investment focused on Hall's wire ropes subsidiary company.

Overton Brothers' Wire Rope Co.Ltd. was a wholly owned subsidiary of Hall's Barton Ropery. Their factory was sited in Beverley, East Yorkshire, and is pictured here in 1935.

The rope industry survived the Great Depression rather better than many heavy engineering industries, with national unemployment averaging 12-22%, around half of the figure for shipbuilding.[36] In the Humber region, local governments attempted to limit the effects of the Depression by setting up job creation projects in which light industry was seen as the solution to the crisis unfolding for large urban employers such as Ruston-Hornsby of Lincoln.[37] Hall's Barton Ropery, at the centre of Barton's industrial hub, represented a crucial source of income for the community and it helped Barton weather the economic storm. Yet times were difficult for Hall's, and in the mid-1930s there were extensive redundancies; remaining staff were usually working on short-time. Due in great part to trading competition from foreign manufacturers, and even from domestic manufacturers in traditionally secure British Colonial markets, the grave situation was eventually relieved in 1936 by Tariff reform. This protected British industry against foreign competition and in the case of rope manufacture, lowered the price of hemp from £250 per ton to less than £90 per ton. A company spokesman seemed relieved with this new economic policy, stating: 'I think we can be quietly optimistic, though at the moment we can only look about a month ahead'.[38]

Hall's expanded their wire rope business during the 1930s, especially in Eastern Europe and South America. This catalogue proudly included letters of recommendation, written in Polish, and photographs of oil wells in Poland which used 'Hallmark' ropes.

Until, the late 1930s, Britain's armed forces remained un-developed, and companies such as Hall's Barton Ropery did not benefit from military orders. Re-armament did eventually occur and, interestingly, the workforce later seems to have regarded the company's War Office production as an immediate prelude to war. One ex-employee recalled the company changing its working day from 9am-4pm to 6am-6pm after Chamberlain's return from appeasement talks in 1938. Even if such a turn-over to re-armament production was not as abrupt as this reminiscence suggests, company records show wire rope sales alone rose from just over £60,000 in 1937 to nearly £80,000 in the following year.[39] When war was finally declared, the company was once again taken under direct control of the War Office, and through the controlled supply of hemp, manila and sisal, continued to provide for military needs. The scale of these contracts was something not experienced before by the company. In 1943 for example, the sales of all kinds of rope and twine approached £250,000. A small, but significant part of these sales was to the civilian market (usually between 20-30%). This was due to the demand for products such as bailer twine, ropes, and hoists that were necessary for agricultural uses which had immense significance in a country suffering from food shortages, and therefore relying on the 'home front' to sustain the war effort. Many uses of rope were similar to those which the company had produced during the Great War, although in the 1940s the needs of the *Ministry of Aircraft Production* and the *Ministry of Supply* featured much more strongly.[40] This included the new-found use of wire cable in the tethering of Barrage Balloons.

'De La Pole House', Hull, was a fine medieval building used as the company's main offices from 1900. Sadly, it was destroyed by bombing during the Second World War.

The Second World War proved much more problematic for the company than the Great War, not least regarding Britain's critical financial situation which led to taxation reaching desperately high levels. The firm paid £12,000 in tax at the peak of production in 1943, compared with only around £100 in 1939. Clearly, fuller order books did not provide the profit in the way it had during previous periods of conflict. The company's numerous appeals against these taxes appear to have been unsuccessful and it was not until the early 1950s that the excess tax was paid back. By far the most dramatic setback of the conflict was the destruction in 1943 of the company's Hull offices, at 'De La Pole' House.[41] The loss of the offices perhaps did not significantly impinge on the company's business, as no production facilities were affected, and maybe the greatest significance of this event, in the eyes of the historian, was the destruction of the great cache of historical artefacts and documents which the company had collected over the years. A smaller fire occurred at the Barton works which did not damage machinery but led to one mill working for many months with no gable wall. Such hardships had to be endured when production could not afford to be affected by closure for repairs. Generally, the company adapted to the circumstances. For example, timber needed for repairs to the works and production of ropewalk apparatus was sourced from local boat building firms that were eligible (unlike Hall's) for the government licenses required to purchase high-quality wood for civilian use.

The common theme of disrupted raw material supply re-appeared during the Second World War. Traditional supplies became difficult to obtain as the U-boat war intensified. Hall's raw materials ledger often recorded 'ship lost' in bright red ink besides expected deliveries. However, the invasion of the Philippine Islands by the Japanese in late 1941 was regarded as the most serious set-back. Surviving records show Hall's manila imports dropped from around 160 tons per month in 1941 to less than 150 tons per *year* in 1942.[42] Manila was a superior material for the making of ropes, but as supplies dwindled, sisal and coir fibres were substituted. In 1942 Hall's Barton Ropery used nearly 1000 tons of sisal, nearly 300% more than before the war. Similarly, use of Indian coir fibre, from the husk of the coconut, doubled between 1940 and 1941.[43] When Italy capitulated in 1944, European hemp supplies once again became accessible.

Revolution in 1919 had denied British access to the greater part of the Russian hemp fields, and the new world order of 1945 posed similar problems. The wartime actions in the Philippines had destroyed most plantations, and in 1946 only 1200 tons of manila was imported, compared to well over 100,000 tons in pre war years.[44] In the Dutch East Indies (modern day Indonesia), independence was declared by a nationalist government. One British trader noted that 'plantations in Sumatra and elsewhere [in Indonesia] are mostly intact, but reports of early shipments are disheartening; many of the large owners being unable to regain possession of their properties'.[45] Indeed, the war fought by the Dutch in Indonesia almost certainly hinged on their desire to keep possession of valuable manila plantations, by then, one of the colony's largest exports. In Britain, hemp supplies remained in government control until reconstruction and political negotiation could bring these foreign sources back to some form of normality. This was a great challenge though and Hall's Barton Ropery, who through Admiralty contracts had always been able to find small caches of manila, found it almost impossible to secure supplies of the material once wartime work ended. In 1946 the company managed to secure only 75 tons of manila, whilst even during the worst years of the war they could expect government-controlled deliveries of around 150 tons per year.[46]

And so we enter the post-war history of the company, a period of optimism for Hall's Barton Ropery and a period in which great efforts were made to meet the new challenges of peacetime. A major aspect of this change came after by the invention and development of synthetic fibre cordage, coupled with a necessity to exploit export markets. This will be discussed in a later chapter. The military uses of rope remained a small part of Hall's business. The orders appear to have been very much sporadic though, and many concentrated on the ability of the works to produce special-order ropes. Foreign governments also utilized the works for particular ropes, and the ropewalk was extended outside to the north to enable ropes of 250 fathoms to be produced.[47] This length, although much longer than a 'standard' rope, was particular to the needs of the United States Navy. [48] Such naval orders were infrequent, and the old ropewalk was used for the last time in 1988. Interestingly, this last synthetic rope was tarred to resemble the rigging ropes of the past, and was destined to be used in the restoration of the world's first iron battleship, *HMS Warrior*.[49] This rope, produced just as *Warrior's* ropes were when she was launched in 1860, was a fitting legacy for a company whose products had for so long being influenced by the needs of war.

5. A Marooned Industry

The story of the rope works in the post-war period has traditionally being associated with great changes, especially the introduction of synthetic ropes. It is true, to a certain extent, that the long decade immediately after the Second World War forced the company to change its customers, its products and its approach. However, the post-war story of rope making at Hall's Barton Ropery was also one of continuity in many processes, with many features of the works remaining as they had since the nineteenth century. It was this curious mix of the old and new that greeted Richard Dimbleby when he visited the Ropery for the BBC radio programme '*Down Your Way*', in December 1950.

BBC Presenter, Richard Dimbleby visited the works in 1950. He is pictured here inspecting a large rope awaiting despatch.

photo - Brian Peeps

The financial position of the Barton Ropery was rather precarious in the immediate post-war period. The managers' correspondence reveals their concerns for the profitability of the company. In 1949-50 for instance, Overton Bros (the wire rope subsidiary company) made a pre-tax profit of around £20,000, whereas Barton works manager, Arthur Hendy, wrote in a letter, 'the [Barton site] presently shows a loss'.[1] It seems much of the success of Overton Bros. was absorbed by the struggling Barton concern. Something had to be done to create long-term profitability at the Barton site.

'*Export or die*,' said Minister of Trade, Harold Wilson, in 1949, thus setting the theme for the post-war period. Hall's Barton Ropery accordingly made great efforts to secure export orders, mainly through tempting agents onto their books with promises of lucrative commissions. Instrumental in developing new customers was A. Roland Dagwell, who later became Director and finally Chairman of the company.[2] The industry in 1950 was unrecognisable from that of 1939, still smarting from the disruption to trade which occurred during wartime. Sisal and manila supplies remained government-controlled until 1948 and 1953 respectively and, accordingly, prices remained volatile.[3] While the supply of raw materials for making natural fibre rope were still disrupted and uncertain we can conclude that development of synthetic fibre rope making was an attempt by the company to create more stability, using raw materials that were less subject to interruption.

Donald Hendy (third from left) enjoyed almost complete independence at the Barton Site, but his attitude to central management (R.Dagwell pictured far left was Chairman) often led to tensions in the company.

photo - Brian Peeps

It seemed the development of synthetic fibre ropes had come from nowhere as its development, perhaps surprisingly, had not taken place to any great extent during wartime. However, once the benefits of waterproof, strong and cheap cordage became apparent, the uses for this rope exploded. Hall's was quick to adopt new technology and from the early 1950s onwards, capital investment at the Barton works consistently favoured synthetic fibre machinery over that used to process natural fibres [4]. Indeed, when the works finally closed in 1989 some of the natural-fibre machinery installed in the early twentieth century was still in use.

A report of the Hard Fibre Cordage Federation outlined the changing nature of the industry and emphasised the increasing reliance of individual manufacturers on repeat customers.[5] In a rare instance where the 'official' narrative matches perfectly with surviving documentary evidence, records show that the company carefully developed lasting (and therefore lucrative) relationships with customers as diverse as Icelandic fisheries and the Pakistani Government.[6] Maintaining these customers 'on the books' was conducted by agents who Hall's made great efforts to court. The importance of these agents are illustrated in a dispute between the company and an agent, Hopkinson's and Co; in which Hopkinson complained that 'before he came on the scene [Hall's Barton Ropery] were not well known in shipping companies and now your name is accepted as being among the principal shipping suppliers even by concerns with whom we may not actually do business'.[7] These suppliers believed Hall's Barton Ropery owed them much of the company's success. However, the company managed to successfully penetrate Middle Eastern, South American and Caribbean markets and only the limited production capacity of the company checked this growth. Many records show that the company was forced to decline offers to provide quotations, especially for lower value synthetic fibres and smaller natural cordages such as twine. In fact, the production of twines became increasingly sidelined in the company's activities, a process that began in 1948 when the company left the binder twine section of the Hard Fibre Cordage Federation.[8] This was probably due to the fact that after wartime agricultural needs had been met, it was no longer profitable for Hall's to continue to make such a low-profit – high-bulk product.

'Hallmark' ropes were sent all around the world, particularly Commonwealth countries. Here a large cable rope is ready for despatch to Rangoon, (now Yangon), Burma.

Through their agents, the company's management carefully cultivated foreign markets. These agents were used to supply briefing notes regarding potential sales opportunities which in turn were dictated by political and geographical issues. A study of these, along with some companion evidence, gives the historian an interesting insight into the management's decision making process. In South America for instance, the company was keen to follow geological surveys that studied the feasibility of mining and oil drilling activities, as these could influence the company's long-term planning strategies by anticipating demand in certain aspects of their business.[9]

Which markets did Hall's attempt to exploit? The company tried to maintain pre-war contacts in the 1950s, but understandably found this difficult in the changed political and economic climate. It is likely that the large Polish oil market, which had proved profitable to the company before the Second World War, remained out of reach behind the Iron Curtain. Hall's Barton Ropery worked hard to maintain contracts in the newly independent Commonwealth countries. Many former colonies such as Pakistan continued to use British colonial specifications for their government supply needs, and indeed the paperwork preserved in the company archive shows a remarkable continuity in administrative procedures before and after its independence. In 1951, the Pakistani Standards Inspector visited the works to ensure ropes were being made to the quality the government required.[10] Throughout the 1950s and 1960s, Commonwealth markets were particularly important for the company and preferential tariffs served to keep Britain's industry heavily invested in these countries. It is clear that Hall's benefited from this government policy.

Beyond government orders, Hall's was also keen to remain an important supplier to private industry in Commonwealth markets. British industry was after all instrumental in the development of commerce in many diverse markets. Iran was occupied by Britain during the Second World War, and the *Anglo-Iranian Petroleum Company* controlled the country's oil industry in the immediate post-war period.[11] Hall's Barton Ropery, like many British companies, was eager to exploit the opportunities this presented, promoting their wire ropes (and to a certain extent natural fibre ropes) to the new oil industry.[12] Similarly, British industry was instrumental in the rapid development of the South American oil and mining industries, and the British companies based there naturally chose British suppliers to meet their needs.[13] So important was this industrial development that in order to secure British industrial interests, the British government supported a coup in Iran to overthrow the elected government which had threatened nationalisation of the oil industry. Iran, was of course just one example of the company's eagerness to engage in the oil industry as records survive of regular contracts with British owned oil companies in Kuwait, Saudi Arabia, Syria, Iraq, Oman and Yemen, and many others throughout the Middle East.[14]

Similarly, British economic influence in the post-war world served to secure supplies of raw materials. With the exploitation of African sisal fibres during the Second World War, the British industry had found an excellent source of raw materials. The supply of these materials was controlled by the *Tanganyika Sisal Marketing Board*, (T.A.S.M.A.) which in their own words would:

> 'Provide a valuable measure of stability to the benefit of all growers in East Africa...
> [and] to the advantage of everyone in the industry.'[15]

This association, formed in 1948, maintained close links with British industry, exporting the vast majority of the sisal it controlled to Britain. In Barton, sisal ropes became popular and compared favourably in cost to the new synthetic fibres. In the early 1950s, Hall's Barton Ropery began to advertise the virtues of sisal rope, chiefly because of its water repellence. Forced on British Rope Manufacturers once manila sources had become blocked in the Second World War, East African sisal was an unexpected success. In the post-war period it was established as a realistic rival to the more expensive manila fibre. Hall's invested in machinery to protect the rope with more sophisticated substances than the traditional tar (although this could still be supplied if requested). They made great store of advertising the scientific new processes used to prevent damage by 'bacteria, funghi [sic], protozoa, algae and other micro organisms'.[16] The language of selling rope had clearly become much more scientific, as evidence of independent tests, common in the wire rope brochures of the 1930s, now became the norm in natural fibre brochures.

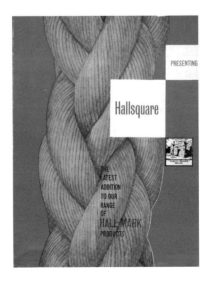

During the 1950s and 60s the company invested in the updating of equipment. 'Hallsquare' ropes were cross-laid, very strong and did not wear out as quickly as traditional ropes. They quickly found favour for nautical uses.

Through the exploitation of these new opportunities the company's post-war future was secured. They steadily modernised, purchasing new machinery throughout the 1950s to replace some which had probably been maintained at the works since the later nineteenth century.[17] Much of this development was focused on the mass-production of synthetic 'standard' ropes, a market that was becoming increasingly competitive as supplies of raw materials began to be more widely available. However, natural fibres remained a company speciality and during the early 1950s Hall's invested in a cross-lay rope making machine to 'plait' ropes which were stronger, lighter and more durable than traditional three or four strand ropes.[18] These found favour on ships where conditions could be very hard on rope. This broadening of the product range was crucial to the company's post-war development plans.

The records which survive from the post-war period, although fragmentary, are quite detailed, and would warrant further work. General conclusions show that Hall's Barton Ropery remained a successful company throughout the 1950s and 1960s, with a renewed emphasis on wire rope production at its Beverley subsidiary company, and new synthetic fibres at Barton. Output of the latter rose significantly during the later 1950s, and in 1959 Hall's Barton Ropery reported the fourth highest growth rate in the industry.[19]

Hall's rigging department, where ropes could be fitted with various eyes, hooks and other hardware, was an important aspect of the business. Here Chairman, Ron Dagwell is seen supervising the renewing of the 'rope' sign. A similar sign can be seen today in the Ropery Coffee Shop.

So how does the post-war story of the rope works fit into the story of the Humber region? After all, even by the end of the Great War the company no longer relied on the industry of Hull and Grimsby for its core of customers. Similarly, the Haven had become silted up by the 1930s, and was rarely used by the rope works even before the outbreak of the Second World War.[20] Hull did still remain the economic focus of the Humber region, and at least part of the company's business relied upon the city as an international port. Indeed the company continued to maintain their headquarter offices in the city, building new offices in New Cleveland Street in 1953.[21] The company's rigging department was convenient for many of Hall's Icelandic and Scandinavian customers, as they often included in their orders the request that the wires and ropes they needed should be fitted to their fishing vessels when they docked in Hull.[22] In correspondence the company seemed eager to emphasise how the location of the rope works could save in time and the cost of shipping.

The case for an industrial development region focused on the Humber had been proposed in the 1930s, and by the 1960s, although politically contentious, the idea had gained momentum.[23] By the late 1960s there were serious government studies into the feasibility of creating a 'Humberside Maritime Industrial Area'; something which was intended to be akin to Rotterdam's 'Europort'.[24] Broadly speaking this concept involved the development of the lower Humber Estuary by 'new' industries, especially in the petrol-chemical sector. Such development had proceeded at a steady rate in the 1950s, resulting in a peak of employment in the region in 1966. The 1969 'Maritime Industrial Area' plan eventually failed as it demanded high capital investment with little attendant increase in employment, the government's main aim for the region. In Barton specifically, both chemical and fertilizer works occupied large acreages, but provided few employment opportunities. Decline in the brick and tile making industry was already occurring. In this context, the development of Scunthorpe's Steel industry also served to draw employment opportunities away from Barton. Hall's Barton Ropery remained a major employer in Barton, and probably accounted for the majority of rope products sold from the region; around 4.5% of the total of all goods produced in Humberside.[25] As a labour-intensive industry it was marooned in an area where increasingly industry was on a much larger scale, even if only in terms of infrastructure. As a traditional industry, Hall's Barton Ropery was in a stronger position than many. The 1970s presented new challenges and new opportunities. Political disputes seriously damaged the fishing industry and must have impacted on the company's business. The oil shocks of the early 1970s probably conspired through the massive over-production of the petro-chemical industry to lower the price of Hall's raw materials which were formed as by-products of oil refining. Production records show the company survived remarkably well through these difficult times, relying on consistent and lucrative contracts from governments and departments such as the NCB and British Steel.[26] Indeed, it appears the early 1970s saw the peak of the company's success, the number of employees rising from around 200 in 1971 to 315 in 1973, the year incidentally, that Donald Hendy died after serving the company since 1927.[27]

A Marooned Industry

Donald B. Hendy, Works Manager and Director (1927-1973).

Hendy, whose family had been associated with the company and town of Barton since 1901, remained very active in the day-to-day management of the Barton Works even after his promotion to director. Thomas Nicholson, works manager under Hendy, maintained his position at Barton after Hendy's death, and was able to develop a more independent managerial style once the works became more directly under his control. A Scotsman who had in fact entered the industry as an apprentice rope maker, Nicholson had spent his previous career with the UK's largest rope manufacturers, British Ropes. Subsequently, his time as works manager saw much change at the Barton site, especially in managerial practices. It appears that rather like Hendy before him, Nicholson valued his independence at Barton, often to the frustration of those who controlled the company's finances in Hull. Indeed, it is often recalled that Nicholson often presented Hull's management with a *fait accompli*, especially in regard to general repair and development of the Barton buildings. Early in his tenure several buildings, including the south end of the ropewalk, were built or rebuilt. These included numerous storage sheds and a new synthetic fibre mill to the east of the original buildings on the site of what was once the Hall's family house, demolished in the 1930s.[28] Those who remember this period recall the refurbishment of older buildings, and the concreting of the floor of the old ropewalk, all of which served to remove much of the 'Victorian' atmosphere from the works.

During the later 1970s, the international standing of Hall's Barton Ropery was under some threat from increases in shipping charges and the dollar falling against sterling. In 1980, the company wrote to one of their suppliers explaining price rises by stating that:

> 'This is out of [our] control…but with your co-operation and our efforts we can surmount these difficulties.'[29]

The situation was made especially difficult with the emergence of newly-industrialised countries in South-East Asia, and concern eventually turned to grudging acceptance that many markets were now blocked-off to the company as foreign competitors closed in. With a sense of resignation detectable, the company's export manager wrote in 1980:

> 'Have contacted our customer. This year's company requirement is only for wire rope. Our competition will be Korean and Japanese so I am not overly optimistic that we have much chance here…'[30]

Such foreign competition was a problem for the company in both export and domestic markets, especially as the sectors of the industry hit hardest by this were wire rope manufacture and general engineering use. British rope manufacturers which specialised in what could be called the 'lighter' type of production including small-gauge yachting, climbing and specialist ropes, were less affected by the increase in imported cordage as many Asian manufacturers were not concerned with such small 'niches' of the market.

It could be argued that what Hall's needed was a 'niche' product, one with appeal beyond the small number of stable markets that the company possessed. During the early 1980s, the company began to diversify into steel wire distribution. Initially this involved sourcing 'raw' wire materials from France for their own use, that being cheaper than UK sourced wire. Eventually Hall's accepted an offer to distribute the French company's wire products, including steel rods used to support reinforced concrete and to make springs for such diverse uses as bus seats and car suspension. This venture, often making the company £40 per ton sold, was profitable and offered a stable financial base for their rope making business. The company maintained their reputation for high-quality traditional ropes, so much so that when a replica seventeenth century sailing ship was constructed in America, Hall's Barton Ropery provided the ropes used to rig it.[31] Such work, although good for securing column inches, was of a very limited use for securing the company's prosperity! Perhaps the greatest strength of Hall's operations lay not with a 'niche' product, but instead with the business practices the firm pursued. Throughout its twentieth century existence Hall's advertising literature emphasised the company's ability to make ropes to order, promising swift delivery. The company was able to do this as there was a high chance that any 'standard' rope would be available ex-stock.[32] In the 1930s the company produced a publication detailing the numerous instances when the company was called upon to 'save the day': the wording was particularly vivid, but emphasised the importance the company placed on been able to fulfil orders with speed:

> 'Some years ago, the Ellerman's Wilson Line had the steamer "Hull" ashore
> off the Yorkshire Coast. Numerous attempts to pull her off had failed. We
> received an order at 10.30 one morning to make a tow-rope of 12" circumference
> for use on this job. We made this rope, fitted it, and delivered it to the dock
> within twelve hours. The rope gave the requisite strain, the ship towed off, and
> was in Hull at 1 o'clock the next morning.'[33]

Although the above extract was taken from a mid-1930s pamphlet, many of its features could still be identified even in the later 1970s. Hall's still possessed a rigging department in Hulls docks and from there was able to prepare ropes to customer's requirements. By the late 1970s this was a relatively rare service for rope makers to provide, and must have been a boon to potential shipping customers. In London, John Black ran a large store for the company's products. One lorry load of rope was sent to London each day during the 1970s, and judging from surviving order books, keeping the London department fully stocked accounted for around 30% of production from Barton.[34]   However, this tangible business asset was surrendered (perhaps unavoidably) during the early 1980s.

Specialist ropes were still produced at Barton during the 1970s and 1980s.
Here a finished rope is taken off the ropewalk through the despatch building, just as it was done when it was constructed in 1807.

photo - courtesy Brian Peeps

John Black had a reputation as an excellent salesman, but, after his death in 1982, a considerable number of the clients he had personally cultivated were lost. Although figures have not survived, employees of the firm often recall that the number of London-bound lorries decreased from one per day to only one per week after this date. This observation has stayed with numerous former employees, and perhaps became an indication of the changing fortunes of the company. In terms of business lost, the impact of Black's death must have been marked. Of course, the company retained agencies with large stocks in Newcastle and overseas, including large fishing agents in Newfoundland, yet it appears that the policy of maintaining high levels of stock was gradually beginning to become untenable for all of the company's agents. As trading conditions became more competitive, large stocks of rope no longer represented 'guaranteed' sales, and hence it was dangerous to have too much stock lying idle. Writing in 1980, the export manager advised a Newfoundland agent:

> 'Certain sizes of manila rope have been in stock for anything up to four years and again you will agree that this is not economical.' [35]

Later in that year he explained:

> 'Any profit on goods held for 12 months on stock has been absorbed in inflation etc because of constantly increasing costs.' [36]

John Black was the London agent for Hall's Barton Ropery, maintaining large stores and co-ordinating sales there.

A Marooned Industry

Whether Hall's were forced to reduce their stock levels due to such outside factors, or whether it was a decision taken with little forethought, the consequences were bordering disastrous, effectively eliminating the 'niche' that the company had secured for itself. Suppliers appear to have been frustrated with Hall's inability to provide for their customers. The company's French wire agreement also failed early in the 1980s again due to the impossibility of holding large stocks. The loss of this lucrative agreement was a further blow to the company's profitability.

A display of **Barton**-made ropes on one of the company's own lorries. In the 1970s, such lorries were making deliveries to agents across the country with a re-assuring regularity. Note the model of the Humber Bridge; such good publicity was difficult to resist, even if the company had little to do with its construction.

photo - Brian Peeps

Although it would be injudicious to describe British Ropes, the largest producer of ropes in the UK, as 'predatory', it had a recognised track record for exploiting the weaknesses of smaller companies. Formed in 1924 from eight smaller firms, it had expanded (and subsequently rationalised through selective closures) throughout the twentieth century.[37] Between 1959 and 1971 the company had purchased twenty-one rope manufacturers, closing each one immediately after purchase.[38] It was clear to Hall's management that British Ropes represented a threat as their ropes' superior production capacity served to place great pressure on the company's markets. In the cases of the National Coal Board, railways and other large industries, Hall's found it increasingly difficult to compete to secure orders. Thus, they had to increasingly rely on existing customers. Repeat customers had always been important, and the company had been proud of its ability to maintain them, but by the 1980s the loss of a single repeat customer had serious implications for the company.[39]

In 1986 Hall's Barton Ropery finally lost their battle to remain independent, although ironically not to British Ropes, the company which had placed the most pressure on their activities. Instead the company was purchased by a Devon firm, Bridport-Gundry Ltd. Established by the

Gundry family in the famous rope making town of Bridport by 1665, the company had become one of the premier rope makers in the country.[40] The motives of Bridport-Gundry's takeover will perhaps never be ascertained; the 'smoking gun' will probably be never found, if any such evidence ever existed. There has been much speculation within the community of Barton as to why this company purchased Hall's Barton Ropery, ranging broadly from the elimination of a competitor to the possibility of an asset stripping operation. Perhaps Bridport-Gundry purchased the company with the intention of entering the markets Hall's had previously dealt in. Certainly Bridport-Gundry was not eliminating a direct competitor in 1986, as they focused mainly on the 'lighter' gauges of rope, especially those used in yachting and fishing. Hall's Barton Ropery didn't make such ropes in any great quantities and Bridport-Gundry could not have exploited Hall's existing customers.

Management was finally brought under Bridport-Gundry's control and Tom Nicholson retired immediately. Michael Dagwell left his position as Managing Director after serving for one year with the new owners. The company inexplicably invested in a new ropewalk at Barton, which, according to former employees, cost several thousand pounds, but was never used to make a single rope. The Ropewalk building itself was last used in 1988 and afterwards remained semi-derelict. During this period there was widespread speculation that the rope works could move to a purpose-built factory. Glanford Borough Council was reported to support the proposed scheme to re-locate the works onto the Humber Bridge Industrial Estate, but how tangible this support was is a matter for intense speculation in Barton even today.[41] Nevertheless, before any long-term plans for Hall's Barton Ropery could be pursued, the company was once again sold. Bridon Plc, as British Ropes was re-named in 1974, finally secured ownership of Hall's Barton Ropery in 1989 and less than one month after the takeover was completed, announced that Barton's works (albeit not the wire rope works in Beverley) would cease production with immediate effect.[42] Centuries of rope making in Barton had come to an abrupt, if not inevitable, conclusion.

Loose Ends

Following the closure of the works in December 1989 a small number of staff was kept on to remove the redundant machinery and scrap anything that remained. Once their work was complete the redundant Ropery buildings remained derelict for some years.

The abandoned ropewalk lay undisturbed for ten years.

In 1994 The Proudfoot Group purchased the site, opening their supermarket store in 1996. Development of the site continued under their ownership when they formed a partnership with North Lincolnshire Council and the Waterside Artists Co-operative in 1999. Funding of £200,000 was obtained to renovate the southern part of the Grade II listed Ropewalk building from Yorkshire Forward, the Single Regeneration Budget, European Regional Development Fund, the Proudfoot Group and North Lincolnshire Council. Ropewalk Contemporary Art & Craft opened in April 2000 offering two galleries, four artists' studios and three workshop rooms.

Development of the remainder of the Ropewalk started in 2005 when £1.2 million was secured from the same sources and additional funds from WREN and Arts Council England to complete the renovation of the whole building. Opening for business in April 2006 the redeveloped building now houses twenty-two businesses and employs forty-six people. The space contains an additional gallery, twelve artists' workspaces, fifteen creative industries units, one larger commercial unit, two meeting rooms and a 120 seat auditorium, the Ropery Hall.

In 2004, the land to the east of the Ropewalk was developed for housing by Peter Ward, and in March 2007 the Despatch Building opened as a Day Spa after considerable renovation, thus extending the regeneration of the wider area.

The Ropewalk is run as a not-for-profit venture with all rental income for twenty years being used to run and maintain the building. With visitors increasing year on year, over 25,000 in 2006, and a developing regional reputation as a centre for high quality visual art, the Ropewalk has now become a centre for excellence in a very different field.

The Heritage project was set up in 2006 with funding from the Heritage Lottery Fund and the Waterside Arts Co-operative. Educational Resources have been produced by Jane Dowden, and as part of this a new Heritage display has been produced. A small archive of Hall's Barton Ropery resources has been collected for future historical research.

This volume's companion, *Family Ties: Stories from Hall's Barton Ropery* is based on the personal recollections of the men and women who worked at the Ropery, and is written and edited by Nick Triplow.

Notes

Introduction.

1) *The Story of Hall's Barton Ropery Co. Ltd.* (Manchester, 1924)

2) *The Story of the Hall-Mark* (Cloister Press, 1975)

3) E. Teeter, 'Techniques and Terminology of Rope-Making in Ancient Egypt', *Journal of Egyptian Archaeology*, Vol. 73 (1987).

4) 'Natural Cordage', <http://www users.cs.york.ac.uk/~mjf/bushcraft/cordage.html >, (21st March, 2007)

5) W. Tyson, *Rope. A History of the Hard Fibre Cordage Industry in the United Kingdom.* (Hard Fibre Cordage Association, 1966) p.6

6) A. Platts, *Land and People in Medieval Lincolnshire* (12 Vols. History of Lincolnshire Committee, 1979, Vol. IV) p. 98 and p.110

7) Lincolnshire Archives Office (LAO), Lincoln, Barton Par , 23/2/3, 'Town Book for the Town and Manor of Barton.' 1676, See also Russell, *The Town Book of Barton Upon Humber,* (Barton-Upon-Humber Branch Worker's Education Association, 1980) for transcript.

8) G. Jackson, *The Trade and Shipping of Eighteenth Century Hull* (East Yorkshire Historical Society, 1975) p.66

9) *Clayton's Hull Directory, 1803* (Hull, 1803) p.16

10) Ropewalk Heritage Project Archive (RHPA), Barton Upon Humber, Private Donations, RHPA/5/ 'The Brick Closes, the property of George Uppleby Esq. and Sarah his Wife. October, 1801'

11) *The Story of the Hall-Mark,* 1975, p.3

12) A.G. Credland, *The Journal of Surgeon Cass. Aboard the Whaler 'Brunswick' of Hull, 1824.* (Humberside Libraries and Arts, 1988) p.4

13) *The Story of the Hall-Mark,* 1975, p.5

14) The Lincoln, Rutland and Stamford Mercury, 10th September, 1852

15) *The Story of the Hall-Mark,* 1975, p.7

16) H.W. Ball, *The Social History and Antiquities of Barton-Upon-Humber,* (Barton Upon Humber, 1856)   p. 20

17) Various sources have been consulted, including Trade Directories, Poll Books, Land Tax Returns and private sources. It is worth noting it is unlikely that *Eagle House,* supposedly built by John Hall in 1829, was in fact his residence. Its owner was probably Mr. Robert Hall, an unrelated merchant of Barton. John Hall lived in 15 Charlotte Street, Sculcoates throughout most of his life.

18) *The Story of Hall's Barton Ropery,* 1924. p.19

19) Ibid.

20) Lincoln, Rutland and Stamford Mercury, 22nd January 1864. And Tyszka, D.M. *The Later History of Barton-Upon Humber: Part Six. Church and People in a Victorian Country Town. Barton Parish 1830-1900* (7 vols. Barton-Upon-Humber Branch of the Workers' Educational Association, 2006) Vol. 6. p. 61

21) Lincoln, Rutland and Stamford Mercury, 5th January, 1855, and respectively, *The Story of the Hallmark,* 1975. p.10

22) J. Bellamy, *The Trade and Shipping of Nineteenth Century Hull.* (East Yorkshire Historical Society, 1971) p.120

23) *The Story of the Hallmark,* 1975, p.16

24) Ibid.

25) Ibid.

26) R. Clapson, *The Later History of Barton Upon Humber, Part4. 'Barton and the River Humber 1086-1900* (7 Vols. Barton Upon Humber Branch Worker's Education Association., 2005) Vol. 4., p.57

27) *The Story of the Hallmark,* 1975, p.18

28) D.R. Mills, (Ed) *Twentieth Century Lincolnshire.* (12 Vols. History of Lincolnshire Committee, 1989. Vol. XII) p.160

29) E. Gillett, *A History of Grimsby.* (Oxford University Press, 1970) and Maskouska, J. *Goole: A Port in Green Fields.* (York, 1973)

30) *The Story of Hall's Barton Ropery,* 1924. p.20

31) Ibid. p.23

32) NELA, Grimsby, UDC/ 81/3/ Minute Books of Barton Upon Humber Urban District Council, 1921-2

33) *The Story of the Hallmark,* 1975, p.18

34) Ibid. p.21

35) Ropewalk Heritage Project Archive (RHPA), Barton, RHPA/1/5, 'Income Tax and Excess Profits Tax. 20th June 1934- 31ST December 1950'

36) RHPA, Barton, RHPA/1/5, 'Income Tax and Excess Profits Tax. 20th June 1934- 31ST December 1950'

37) *The Story of the Hallmark,* 1975, p.22

38) Ibid. p. 23

39) RHPA, Barton, Proudfoot Deposit, RHPA/3/20. *Hallmark Manila Ropes.*

40) RHPA, Barton, RHPA/6/1-9 Production Records, and North East Lincolnshire Archives, Grimsby, 1184/ Records of Hall's Barton Ropery Co. Ltd.

41) A thorough search of the Royal Geographic Society Archive, Greenwich, (EE/ Everest Expeditions) has proved fruitless.

42) Scunthorpe Evening Telegraph, 29th January, 1971

43) *The Story of the Hallmark,* 1975, p.22

44) P.N. Jones, and others (ed.), *A Dynamic Estuary: Man, Nature and the Humber.* (Hull, 1988) p.156

45)   RHPA, Barton, RHPA/6/1-9 Production Records, and North East Lincolnshire Archives, Grimsby, 1184/ Records of Hall's Barton Ropery Co. Ltd.

46) RHPA, Barton, RHPA/6/1-9 Production Records, and North East Lincolnshire Archives, Grimsby, 1184/ Records of Hall's Barton Ropery Co. Ltd.

47) Scunthorpe Evening Telegraph, 29th December, 1989

Chapter I-
The Foundation of Hall's Ropery.

1) *The Story of the Hall-Mark* (Cloister Press, 1975) p. 2

2) Lincolnshire Archives Office (LAO), Lincoln, Barton Par , 23/2/3, 'Town Book for the Town and Manor of Barton.' 1676, Also see Russell, R. *The Town Book of Barton Upon Humber,* (Barton-Upon-Humber Branch Worker's Education Association, 1980) for transcript.

3) LAO. Lincoln, INV.8/389 B, Wm. Seller, Roper, 1540

4) G. Jackson. *Hull in the Eighteenth Century. A Study in Economic and Social History.* (Oxford University Press, 1972) p.57

5) S. Ville. 'The Growth of Specialization in English Shipowning, 1750-1850 (*The Economic History Review, New Series, Vol.46, No. 4 (Nov., 1993)* p.704

6) Jackson, *Hull in the Eighteenth Century.* p.141

7) Jackson, *Hull in the Eighteenth Century.* p.181

8) *Battle's Hull Directory, 1791.* (Hull, 1791) p.16

9) *The Story of Hall's Barton Ropery Co. Ltd.* (Manchester, 1924) rear inside cover.

10) J. Bellamy. *The Trade and Shipping of Nineteenth Century Hull.* (East Yorkshire Historical Society, 1971) p.53

11) *The Story of the Hall-Mark* (1975). p.12-13

12) Bellamy, *The Trade and Shipping of Nineteenth Century Hull.* p.9

13) A. Storey. *Trinity House of Kingston Upon Hull.* 2.Vols., (Trinity House, 1967 & 1969) Vol. II, p. 47

14) Hull City Archives (HCA), Hull, 'Papers relating to the hire of ships for use as transports for the commissioners of H.M. Transport Office, 1795', DBX/12/10, 'Charter parties using Commissions printed from: *Aurora* of Hull, John Hall, Master.'

15) R. Larn & B. Larn. *The Shipwreck index of the British Isles- The East Coast of England.* (9 Vols. Lloyds Register of Shipping, 1997) vol. 3 p.220.

16) R. Russell. *The Enclosure of Barton Upon Humber.* (Barton Upon Humber Branch Worker's Education Association, 1968) p.12

17) LAO, Lincoln, Barton Parish Deposit 17/2, Barton Enclosure award 1797.

18) R. Clapson. *The Later History of Barton Upon Humber, Part4. 'Barton and the River Humber 1086-1900* (Barton Upon Humber Branch Worker's Education Association., 2005) p.45

19) The Lincoln, Rutland and Stamford Mercury, 21st June, 1800

20) Ropewalk Heritage Project Archive (RHPA), Barton Upon Humber, Private Donations, RHPA/5/ 'The Brick Closes, the property of George Uppleby Esq. and Sarah his Wife. October, 1801'

21) H. Calvert. *A History of Kingston Upon Hull.* (Phillmore, 1978) p.234

22) Jackson, *Hull in the Eighteenth Century.* p.78

23) W. Tyson. *Rope. A History of the Hard Fibre Cordage Industry in the United Kingdom.* (Hard Fibre Cordage Association, 1966) p.137

24) *The Story of Hall's Barton Ropery.* (1924) rear inside cover.

25) A.G. Credland. *The Journal of Surgeon Cass. Aboard the Whaler 'Brunswick' of Hull, 1824.* (Humberside Libraries and Arts, 1988) p.13

26) *The Story of the Hall-Mark* (1975). p.9

27) R.S. Porter (ed.) *Unpathed Waters – Account of the Life of Captain Joseph Huddart FRS* (Quiller Press, London 1989) p.102

28) Storey. *Trinity House of Kingston Upon Hull.* Vol. I, p.86.

29) Ball, *The Social History and Antiquities of Barton-Upon-Humber,* p. FIND

30) *The Story of the Hall-Mark* (1975). p.5

31) Clapson, *'Barton and the River Humber 1086-1900* p. 98

32) *The Gourock Ropeworks Company Limited.* (Glasgow, undated) p.9

Chapter II-
Ropemakers. The Making of Industrial Barton

1) H.W. Ball. *The Social History and Antiquities of Barton-Upon-Humber,* (Barton Upon Humber, 1856) p.20

2) Ibid. p.20

3) *The Story of the Hall-Mark* (Cloister Press, 1975) p. 10

4) R. Holdsworth and B. Lavery. *The Ropery Visitor Handbook. The Historic Dockyard, Chatham.* (Chatham Dockyard, 1991) p.4

5) *The Ropery Visitor Handbook, Chatham.* p.7

6) Census of Barton-Upon-Humber, Parish of St. Mary and St. Peter, 1851

7) W. Tyson. *Rope. A History of the Hard Fibre Cordage Industry in the United Kingdom.* (Hard Fibre Cordage Association, 1966) p.121

8) LAO, Lincoln, Barton Parish Deposit, 23/12, 'Minute Books Relating to the Introduction of Gas Lighting to the Town of Barton.'

9) The Lincoln, Rutland and Stamford Mercury, 25th February, 1853.

10) W. Fenton. *Ropeworks. A Brief History of Hall's Barton Ropery.* (Fathom Press, 2007) p. 15

11) R. Russell. *The Town and the People. Part Two, Barton on Humber in the 1850's.* (4 Vols. Barton Upon Humber Branch Worker's Education Association, Vol2, 1978) p.5

12) J.D. Chambers. 'Enclosure and Labour Supply in the Industrial Revolution' (*The Economic History Review, New Series, Vol. 5, No' 3 (1953)* p.320

13) Fenton, *Ropeworks.* P.15

14) Chambers. 'Enclosure and Labour Supply in the Industrial Revolution' p. 328

15) Hallmark, 1974, p. 15

16) A.W. Fox, *Royal Commission on Agriculture: Report on Lincolnshire.* C. 7671, 1895. Many historians have worked on the issue of rural wages, including locally, Rex Russell in *Revolt in the Field,* 1958 and more general works by Joan Thirsk, most notably, *English Peasant Farming, An Agrarian History of Lincolnshire from Tudor to Recent Times,* 1959.

17) J.H. Bellerby, *Agriculture and Industry; Relative Income* (Macmillan) p.210

18) Stamford Mercury, 25th February, 1853.

19) Stamford Mercury, 27th February, 1852.

20) R. Russell. *Cradle to Grave. Part Four, Barton on Humber in the 1850's.* (4 Vols. Barton Upon Humber Branch Worker's Education Association, Vol4, 1984. p.96

21) Ibid. p.96 and Stamford Mercury, 22nd January, 1864

22) Russell, *Cradle to Grave*. p.70

23) Tyson, *Rope*. p. 138

24) LAO, Lincoln, Barton Parish Deposit, 23/20/1, 'Parish Priest's Visitation Registers. Volume I.'

25) Census of Barton-Upon-Humber, St. Mary. 1861

26) R. Russell. *Great changes in Barton 1793-1900, enclosure, population, schools and Methodism. The Later History of Barton Upon Humber, Part Three.* (4 Vols. Barton Upon Humber Branch Worker's Education Association, Vol. 3, 2002) p.110

27) *The Story of the Hall-Mark*. p. 10

28) P. Lane, N. Raven, & D. Snell. (Eds) *Women, Work and Wages in England 1600-1850.* (Woodbridge, 2004) p.120

29) Tyson, *Rope*. p. 11

30) J. Bellamy. *The Trade and Shipping of Nineteenth Century Hull.* (East Yorkshire Historical Society, 1971) p.21

31) A.M. Urdank. 'Custom, Conflict, and Traditional Authority in the Gloucester Weaver Strike of 1825. (*Journal of British Studies, Vol. 25. No. 2 (Apr 1986)* p.193

32) Tyson, *Rope*. p. 49

33) E.A. Wrigley, and R.S. Schofield. *The Population History of England, 1541-1871. A Reconstruction.* (Cambridge University Press, 1989)

34) Russell, *Cradle to Grave*. p.7

35) T.W. Beastall. *History of Lincolnshire Volume VIII. The Agricultural Revolution in Lincolnshire.* (10 Vols, History of Lincolnshire committee, 1978) Vol. VIII

36) LAO, Lincoln, Lindsey Quarter Sessions. 'LQS, Land Tax, Yarborough Wapentake, Barton-Upon-Humber.' 1884, 1887 and 1888

Chapter III-
Women in the Ropeworks.

1) Tyson, W. *Rope. A History of the Hard Fibre Cordage Industry in the United Kingdom.* (Hard Fibre Cordage Association, 1966) p.38

2) Beastall, T.W. *History of Lincolnshire Volume VIII. The Agricultural Revolution in Lincolnshire.* (12 Vols, History of Lincolnshire committee, 1978) Vol. VIII p.108

3) Lane, P. Raven, N. & Snell, D. (Eds) *Women, Work and Wages in England 1600-1850.* (Woodbridge, 2004) p.84

4) *The Story of Hall's Barton Ropery Co. Ltd.* (Manchester, 1924) p.13

5) Roberts, E. *Women's Work 1840-1940.* (Macmillan, 1968) p.16

6) 'A Day at a Leeds Flax Mill' *The Penny Magazine of the Society For the Diffusion of Useful Knowledge,* Vol. 12, (April 1843) p.504

7) Roberts, *Women's Work.* p.23

8) Ibid. p. 13

9) 5&6 Victoria, Cap.99, Coal Mines Act. (1842)

10) 'A Day at a Leeds Flax Mill', 1843 p.504

11) *History Gazetteer & Directory of Lincolnshire. 1842.* (Sheffield, 1842)

12) 'A Day at a Leeds Flax Mill', 1843 p.505

13) Ibid. p.507

14) Ibid. p.503

15) 'A Day at a Rope and Sailcloth Factory' *The Penny Magazine of the Society For the Diffusion of Useful Knowledge,* Vol. XI, (November 1842) p.465

16) Roberts, *Women's Work.* p.33

17) 'A Day at a Leeds Flax Mill', 1843. p.508

18) Boot, H.M. 'How Skilled Were Lancashire Cotton Factory Workers in 1833?' *The Economic History Review,* New Series, Vol. 48., No.2. (May, 1995) pp.291

19) Ibid. p.285

20) Ibid.

21) *Labour: Women's Employment.* Sessional Papers, c.6894.xxiii. (HMSO, 1894)

22) LAO, Lincoln. Barton Parish Deposit, 23/20/2, 'Parish Priests Visiting Register. Volume 2.'

23) Tyson, W. *Rope. A History of the Hard Fibre Cordage Industry in the United Kingdom.* (Hard Fibre Cordage Association, 1966) p.45

24) Ibid. p.38

25) Ibid.

26) Wrightman, C. *More than Munitions: Women, work and the engineering industries, 1900-1950* (Longman, 1989) p.187

27) Ibid. p.26

28) North East Lincolnshire Archives (NELA), Grimsby, Records of Hall's Barton Ropery Limited, Barton-Upon-Humber, 1184/11, 'Monofilament, Miscellaneous Papers.'

Chapter IV,
War and the Ropery. Problems and Opportunities.

1) Ball, H.W. *The Social History and Antiquities of Barton-Upon-Humber,* (Barton Upon Humber, 1856)   p.21

2) Gillett, E. *A History of Grimsby.* (Oxford University Press, 1970) p.29

3) Hull Advertiser, 28th May, 1807

4) Gillett, E. *A History of Grimsby.* P. 29

5) HCA, Hull, DBX/12/10, Papers relating to the hire of ships for use as transports by the commissioners of HM Transport office, 1795. 'Charter parties using the Commissions printed from: Aurora of Hull, John Hall master'

6) *The Story of Hall's Barton Ropery Co. Ltd.* (Manchester, 1924) p.14

7) Clapson, R. *The Later History of Barton Upon Humber, Part 4. 'Barton and the River Humber 1086-1900* (Barton Upon Humber Branch Worker's Education Association., 2005) p.98

8) 'A Day at a Rope and Sailcloth Factory' *The Penny Magazine of the Society For the Diffusion of Useful Knowledge,* Vol XI, (November 1842) p.466

9) Stamford Mercury, 23rd June, 1854

10) Starkey, D.J. *British Privateering Enterprise in the Eighteenth Century.* (University of Exeter Press, 1990), illustrative of current academic work on this fascinating subject.

11) Tyson, W. *Rope. A History of the Hard Fibre Cordage Industry in the United Kingdom.* (Hard Fibre Cordage Association, 1966) p. 16

12) *The Story of Hall's Barton Ropery Co. Ltd.,* p.20

13) RHPA, Barton, Proudfoot Deposit, RHPA/3/20. *Hallmark Manila Ropes.*

14) National Archives, Kew, CO323/648/80. 'SS Erato. Provision of further information regarding Puglia Steam Navigation Company, with a copy of their original order, in connection with a request to deliver two coils of wire rope, unloaded from SS *Erato* at Malta, to the company Hall's Barton Ropery Company Limited, Hull,' Folio 482-488

15) *The Story of Hall's Barton Ropery Co. Ltd.,* p.24

16) Tyson, *Rope.* p.15

17) Ibid. p.17

18) Crowther, E.M. *Lowe's Rope & Twine Manufactory. A Local Industry.* (Occasional Paper No1, Bewdley Historical Research Group, 1998) p.21

19) Tyson, *Rope.* p.35

20) Ibid. p. 28

21) *The Story of Hall's Barton Ropery Co. Ltd.,* p.29

22) Ibid. p. 23

23) Fenton, *Ropeworks*

24) Tyson, *Rope.* p.52

25) Ibid.

26) RHPA, Barton, Proudfoot Deposit, RHPA/3/66, 'Keep Clear of the Wire Rope Ring.'

27) 'BSI History', undated, <http://www.bsi-global.com/en/Standards-and-Publications/About-British-Standards/History > (7th March, 2007)

28) RHPA, Barton, Proudfoot Deposit, RHPA/3/20, *Hallmark Manila Ropes.*

29) RHPA, Barton, Proudfoot Deposit, RHPA/3/57, *Wire Ropes. How They Are Made.*

30) *The Story of the Hall-Mark* (Cloister Press, 1975) p.17

31) RHPA, Barton, Proudfoot Deposit, RHPA/3/57, *Wire Ropes. How They Are Made.*

32) *The Story of the Hall-Mark,* p.19

33) RHPA, Barton, Proudfoot Deposit, RHPA/3/63, 'Hall's Barton Ropery Co Ltd. Wire Ropes.' Sales Catalogue.

34) *The Story of the Hall-Mark,* p.21

35) RHPA, Barton, RHPA/1/5, 'Income Tax and Excess Profits Tax. 20th June 1934- 31ST December 1950'

36) Tyson, *Rope,* p.39

37) Wright, N.R. *History of Lincolnshire Volume XI. Lincolnshire Towns and Industry* (12 Vols, History of Lincolnshire committee, 1978) Vol. XI. p.49

38) North Lincolnshire Museum, Scunthorpe, 'Rope Industry at Barton Picks up again.' Scunthorpe Evening Telegraph, undated cutting, c.1937-39

39) RHPA, Barton, RHPA/1/5 'Income Tax and Excess Profits tax, 1934-50'

40) RHPA, Barton, RHPA/1/5, 'Income Tax and Excess Profits tax, 1934-50'

41) *The Story of the Hall-Mark,* p.21

42) RHPA, Barton, RHPA/6/13, 'Hemp Book' 1936-46.

43) RHPA, Barton, RHPA/6/13, 'Hemp Book' 1936-46.

44) Nash, G. *'Taking it Green'. The Story of a Great Adventure.* (Belfast Ropeworks Company Limited, 1946) p.14

45) Ibid.

46) RHPA, Barton, RHPA/6/13, Hemp Contracts, 1936-1946.

47) Scunthorpe Telegraph, 20th June, 1969

48) RHPA, Barton, RHPA/6/6, 'Invoice to Dir. of Storage and transportation, Defence Depot, Memphis, TN. USA.'

49) N. Triplow, *Family Ties. Stories from Hall's Barton Ropery* (Fathom Press, 2007) p.71. Further information on HMS Warrior can be found here, <http://www.hmswarrior.org > (4th April, 2007)

Chapter V-
 A Marooned Industry

1) NELA, Grimsby, HBR co. Ltd., 1184/1, Director's correspondence. 16th April 1951 and 28th June 1951

2) *The Story of the Hall-Mark* (Cloister Press, 1975) p.22

3) NELA, Grimsby, HBR co Ltd, 1184/3, Meeting Papers and Minutes.

4) NELA, Grimsby, HBR co. Ltd, 1184/5, Annual Financial Papers

5) 'Report on the supply of Hard Fibre Cordage' (Competition Commission, HMSO, 1956) p.14

6) NELA, Grimsby, HBR co. Ltd, 1184/3, Meeting Papers and Minutes.

7) NELA, Grimsby, HBR co. Ltd, 1184/3, Meeting Papers and Minutes.

8) 'Report on the supply of Hard Fibre Cordage' p.48

9) NELA, Grimsby, HBR co. Ltd, 1184/2, Director's Correspondence.

10) NELA, Grimsby, HBR co. Ltd, 1184/3, Meeting Papers and Minutes

11) Ghaffari, M. *The Political Economy of Oil in Iran.* (London, 2000) p.7

12) RHPA, Barton, Proudfoot Deposit, RHPA/3/42, 'National Iranian Oil Company Commercial Services Group, Iran- Request for Quotation.'

13) Robertson, D.H. *Britain in the World Economy* (Allen & Unwin, 1954) p.177

14) NELA, Grimsby, HBR co. Ltd, 1184/11, Production Records.

15) RHPA, Barton, Proudfoot Deposit, RHPA/3//51, '*TASMA. Tenth Anniversary, 1948-1958*'

16) RHPA, Barton, Proudfoot Deposit, RHPA/3//28, 'Leaflet on L.P Proofed Sisal Rope. Rot Proof- Water Repellent.'

17) NELA, Grimsby, HBR co. Ltd, 1184/5, Annual Financial Papers

18) RHPA, Barton, Proudfoot Deposit, RHPA/3/39, ''Hallsquare' Addition to Hall's Range of Ropes.'

19) NELA, Grimsby, HBR co. Ltd, 1184/3, Meeting Papers and Minutes, 'Statement of Progress for six months ended 30th June 1959.'

20) Newton, R. *My Childhood Playground.* (Hutton Press, 2001) p.172

21) *The Story of the Hall-Mark,* 1975, p. 21

22) East Yorkshire Archives (EYA), Beverley, Hall's Barton Ropery Ltd, Rope Manufacturers, Barton Upon Humber, Records, ddx922/5, File Relating to Mr. Richard Theodors, Iceland, Letter 22nd July 1962

23) Jones, P.N and others (ed.), *A Dynamic Estuary: Man, Nature and the Humber.*(Hull, 1988) p.116

24) Ibid, p.153

25) Ibid, p.151

26) RHPA, Barton, Production Records, RHPA/6/3, 'Rope Makers Instructions.' 1966-1977

27) RHPA, Barton, Financial papers, RHPA/1/2, Directors Report, Year ended 30th June 1973.

28) RHPA, Barton, Buildings and Machinery, RHPA/7/ 2, 'Ropery Plan'

29) RHPA, Barton, Correspondence, RHPA/4/4, Telegram 30th April, 1980

30) RHPA, Barton, Correspondence, RHPA/4/5, Telegram 2nd October, 1980

31) Scunthorpe Evening Telegraph, 29th January 1971.

32) RHPA, Barton, Proudfoot Deposit, RHPA/3/54, British Binder Twine, leaflet.

33) RHPA, Barton, Proudfoot Deposit, RHPA/3/20, Hallmark Manila Rope. p.6

34) RHPA. Barton, Production Records, RHPA/6/3 'Rope Makers Instructions.' 1966-1977

35) RHPA, Barton, Correspondence, RHPA/4/4, Telegram 30th April, 1980

36) RHPA, Barton, Correspondence, RHPA/4/4, Telegram 5th May, 1980

37) Tyson, W. *Rope. A History of the Hard Fibre Cordage Industry in the United Kingdom.* (Hard Fibre Cordage Association, 1966) p. 76

38) Doncaster Archives Department, Doncaster, Bridon Plc, Rope Manufacturers, DY/BRI.

39) RHPA, Barton, Correspondence, RHPA/4/4, Telegram 17th June, 1981

40) Tyson, *Rope*, p. 11

41) Scunthorpe Evening Telegraph, 29th December, 1989

42) Ibid.

Bibliography

The Following brief bibliography is intended to provide some starting points for those who wish to further research the fascinating history of Hall's Barton Ropery, and its place in Barton's industrial heritage.

Manuscript Sources

Doncaster Archives Department, Doncaster, DY/ BRI/ Bridon, Plc.

East Yorkshire Archives, Beverley, DDX 922/ Record's or Hall's Barton Ropery Co Ltd.

EYA, Beverley, Parish Registers, Sculcoates and Hull.

Hull City Archives, Hull, zDDX89/ Documents relating to the Schofield Family

HCA, Hull, WT/ The Charterhouse Deposit.

HCA, Hull, DPD/ Files of the North Eastern Railway Estate Surveyor at York

HCA, Hull, DBX/12/ Papers relating to the hire of ships for use as transports for the commissioners of H.M. Transport Office, 1795'

Lincolnshire Archives Office, Lincoln, Barton Par Deposit

LAO, Lincoln, Parish Registers, Barton-Upon-Humber

LAO, Lincoln, Misc Don/ 492

LAO, Lincoln, LQS/ Land Tax/ Yarborough/ 1805-1889/ Barton On Humber

LAO, Lincoln, FL MISC/

LAO, Lincoln, B.H/ Barton upon Humber.

National Archives, Kew, CO323/ Colonial Office records

NELA, Grimsby, 1184/ Record's of Hall's Barton Ropery Co. Ltd.

NELA, Grimsby, UDC/ 81/3/ Minute Books of Barton Upon Humber Urban District Council

Royal Geographic Archive, Greenwich, EE/ Everest Expeditions

Published Primary sources

Board of Trade. Labour Department. *Accounts of Expenditure of Wage-Earning Women and Children.* Sessional Papers, Vol. LXXXIX (HMSO, 1911)

'Report on the supply of Hard Fibre Cordage' (Competition Commission, HMSO, 1956)

A.W. Fox, *Royal Commission on Agriculture: Report on Lincolnshire.* C. 7671, 1895

Turner, W. *A Guide to Hull,* (Hull, 1805)

Greenwood, J. *A Picture of Hull.* (Hull, 1835)

Pigot & Co'. National Commercial Directory for 1829. Northern & Midland Counties. (Sheffield, 1828)

Too numerous to list here are the various Trade Directories for Lincolnshire and Yorkshire by Pigot, Kelly, White &c. All are locally available at archives and Libraries.

Rope and Rope Yarn, Encyclopaedia Britannica, 1st ed., 1771, page 210-221.
Rope Making, English Encyclopedia, 1867, pp. 420-425

Rope-Making, *Rees's Cyclopaedia, 1819*

'The Case of the Rope-Makers of London', *Broadside,* (London, 1700)

Ball, H.W. *The Social History and Antiquities of Barton-Upon-Humber,* (Barton Upon Humber, 1856)

'A Day at a Leeds Flax Mill' *The Penny Magazine of the Society For the Diffusion of Useful Knowledge,* Vol. XII, (April 1843) pp.501-508

'A Day at a Rope and Sailcloth Factory' *The Penny Magazine of the Society For the Diffusion of Useful Knowledge,* Vol. XI, (November 1842) pp.465-472

Hemp. *Manufacturer and Builder, Vol. 1 (1869)*

Enormous Rope, *Manufacturer and Builder, Vol. 1 (1869)*

Chapman, W. Specification of the Patent Granted to Mr. William Chapman for a Method of Laying, Twisting, or Making Ropes and Cordage. *The Repertory of Arts and Manufactures, Vol. 9 (1798) pp.570-618*

Curr, J. Specification of the Patent Granted to John Curry for a Method of Forming and Making a Flat Rope. *The Repertory of Arts and Manufactures, Vol. 10 (1799)* pp. 620-626

Kendral, W. *Specification of the Patent Granted to Mr. John Kendrew and Mr. Thomas Porthouse for a New Mill or Machine, Upon New Principles, for Spinning Yarn from Hemp, Tow, Flax, or Wool.* The Repertory of Arts and Manufactures, Vol. 16 (1802)

Mitchell, J. Specification of the Patent granted to Mr. James Mitchell for a Method of Manufacturing Cables, Hawsers, or Shroud-Laid Ropes, and Other Cordages, on a Scientific Principle, *The Repertory of Arts and Manufactures, Vol. 11 (1799)*

The Poll Book for Parts of Lindsey in the County of Lincoln. 1823, 1832, 1841, 1852 &c, until the advent of the secret ballot in 1872.

The Story of Hall's Barton Ropery Co. Ltd. (Manchester, 1924)

The Story of the Hall-Mark (Cloister Press, 1975)

The Gourock Ropeworks Co. Ltd.. (Glasgow, 1936)

Nash, G. *'Taking it Green'. The Story of a Great Adventure.* (Belfast Ropeworks Company Limited, 1946)

Wire Ropes. How They Are Made. (Hall's Barton Ropery Co. Ltd., c.1935)

Hallmark Manila Ropes. (Hall's Barton Ropery, undated.)

Published Secondary Sources

Beastall, T.W. *History of Lincolnshire Volume VIII. The Agricultural Revolution in Lincolnshire.* (12 Vols, History of Lincolnshire committee, 1978) Vol. VIII

Bellamy, J. *The Trade and Shipping of Nineteenth Century Hull.* (East Yorkshire Historical Society, 1971)

Bellamy J. *Some Aspects of the economy of Hull in the nineteenth century, with Special Reference to Business History: Being a Thesis Submitted for the Degree of Doctor of Philosophy.* (Hull University, 1965)

Bellamy, J.M. "Cotton Manufacture in Hull" in *Business History*, (Vol. IV, No' 2. 1962, pp91-108)

Benenson, H. 'Patriarchal Constraints on Women Workers' Mobilization: The Lancashire Female Cotton Operatives.' *The British Journal of Sociology*, vol.44., No. 4. (Dec., 1993) p.613-663

Boot, H.M. 'How Skilled were Lancashire Cotton Factory Workers in 1833?' *The Economic History Review*, New Series, Vol. 48., No.2. (May, 1995) pp.283-303

Calvert, H. *A History of Kingston Upon Hull.* (Phillmore, 1978)

Carter, H.R. (ed.) *Modern Flax, Hemp and Jute Spinning and Twisting.'* (London, 1925)

Chambers, J.D. 'Enclosure and Labour Supply in the Industrial Revolution' (*The Economic History Review, New Series, Vol. 5, No' 3 (1953) pp.319-343*)

Clapson, R. *The Later History of Barton Upon Humber, Part 4. 'Barton and the River Humber 1086-1900* (Barton Upon Humber Branch Worker's Education Association., 2005)

Credland, A.G. *The Journal of Surgeon Cass. Aboard the Whaler 'Brunswick' of Hull, 1824.* (Humberside Libraries and Arts, 1988)

Crowther, E.M. *Lowe's Rope & Twine Manufactory. A Local Industry.* (Occasional Paper No1, Bewdley Historical Research Group, 1998)

De Moor, D.E., Starkey, D.J. and Eyck Van Heslinga, E. (Ed.) *Pirates and Privateers: New Perspectives on the War on Trade in the Eighteenth and Nineteenth Centuries.* (University of Exeter Press, 1997)

Drake, M. (ed.) *Population Studies From Parish Registers. A Selection of Readings From 'Local Population Studies.'* (Local Population Studies, 1982)

East, W.G. 'The Port of Kingston-Upon-Hull During the Industrial Revolution. (*Economical, May 1931. pp190-212*)

Ghaffari, M. *The Political Economy of Oil in Iran.* (London, 2000)

Gillett, E. *A History of Grimsby.* (Oxford University Press, 1970)

Gordon, J. *Hull in the Eighteenth Century. A Study in Economic and Social History.* (Hull University Press, 1979)

Hopkins, E. 'Small Town Aristocrats of Labour and Their Standard of Living, 1840-1914' *(The Economic History Review, New Series. Vol. 28, No' 2 (May 1975) pp 222-242)*

Himmelfarb, D. *The Technology of Cordage Fibres and Rope.* (London, 1957)

Jackson, G. *The Trade and Shipping of Eighteenth Century Hull* (East Yorkshire Historical Society, 1975)

Jackson, G. *Hull in the Eighteenth Century. A Study in Economic and Social History.* (Oxford University Press, 1972)

Jones, P.N and others (ed.), *A Dynamic Estuary: Man, Nature and the Humber.* (Hull, 1988)

Lane, P. Raven, N. & Snell, D. (Eds) *Women, Work and Wages in England 1600-1850.* (Woodbridge, 2004)

Larn, R & Larn, B. *The Shipwreck index of the British Isles- The East Coast of England.* (9 Vols. Lloyds Register of Shipping, 1997) vol. 3

Lawrie, G. *The Practical Ropemaker.* (Carter Publications, Belfast, 1948)

MacGregor, D.R. *Merchant Sailing Ships 1815-1850. The Supremacy of Sail* (Conway Maritime Press, 1984)

MacGregor, D.R. *Merchant Sailing Ships 1775-1815* (Model and Allied Publications, 1980)

Maskouska, J. *Goole: A Port in Green Fields.* (York, 1973)

McFarlane, S.B. (ed.) *The Technology of Synthetic Fibres.* (New York, 1953)

Mills, D.R. (Ed) *Twentieth Century Lincolnshire.* (12 Vols. History of Lincolnshire Committee, 1989. Vol. XII) p.160

Newton, R. *My Childhood Playground.* (Hutton Press, 2001)

Pyne, W.H. *Microcosm: Or a Picturesque Delineation of the Arts, Agriculture, Manufactures, &c. of Great Britain.* (10 Vols. 1808. reprint, Luton, 1975) Vol. I.

Roberts, E. *Women's Work 1840-1940.* (Macmillan, 1968)

Robertson, D.H. *Britain in the World Economy* (Allen & Unwin, 1954)

Russell, R. (Eds) *The Town Book of 1676* (Barton Upon Humber Branch Worker's Education Association, 1980)

Russell, R. *The Town and the People. Part Two, Barton on Humber in the 1850's.* (4 Vols. Barton Upon Humber Branch Worker's Education Association, Vol2, 1978)

Russell, R *Parish and Government Part Three, Barton on Humber in the 1850's.* (4 Vols. Barton Upon Humber Branch Worker's Education Association, Vol3, 1978

Russell, R. *Cradle to Grave. Part Four, Barton on Humber in the 1850's.* (4 Vols. Barton Upon Humber Branch Worker's Education Association, Vol4, 1984

Russell, R. *Landscape Changes in South Humberside, The Enclosures of Thirty-Seven Parishes* (Humberside Leisure Services. 1982)

Russell, R. *The Enclosure of Barton Upon Humber.* (Barton Upon Humber Branch Worker's Education Association, 1968)

Russell, R. *Great changes in Barton 1793-1900, enclosure, population, schools and Methodism. The Later History of Barton Upon Humber, Part Three.* (4 Vols. Barton Upon Humber Branch Worker's Education Association, Vol. 3, 2002)

Russell, R. *Sedition, Insurrection and Invasion. The French Revolution in Lincolnshire History.* (Barton Upon Humber Branch Worker's Education Association, 1997)

Schofield, E. *Humber Keels and Keelmen* (Hull, 1992)

Ryan, A.N. 'Trade with the Enemy in Scandinavian and Baltic Ports.' *Transactions of the Royal Historical Society,* 5th *Series, Vol. XII (1962) pp.129-32*

Starkey, D.J. *British Privateering Enterprise in the Eighteenth Century.* (University of Exeter Press, 1990)

Storey, A. *Trinity House of Kingston Upon Hull.* 2. Vols., (Trinity House, 1967 & 1969)

Thirsk, J. *English Peasant Farming, An Agrarian History of Lincolnshire from Tudor to Recent Times,* (Routledge, 1959)

Tyson, W. *Rope. A History of the Hard Fibre Cordage Industry in the United Kingdom.* (Hard Fibre Cordage Association, 1966)

Tyszka, D.M. *The Later History of Barton-Upon Humber: Part Six. Church and People in a Victorian Country Town. Barton Parish 1830-1900* (7 vols. Barton-Upon-Humber Branch of the Workers' Educational Association, 2006) Vol. 6.

Urdank, A.M. 'Custom, Conflict, and Traditional Authority in the Gloucester Weaver Strike of 1825. (*Journal of British Studies, Vol. 25. No. 2 (Apr 1986) pp.193-226*)

Ville, S. 'The Growth of Specialisation in English Shipowning, 1750-1850 (*The Economic History Review, New Series, Vol.46, No. 4 (Nov., 1993) p702-722*)

Waterways and Railways of Barton Upon Humber and New Holland. (Lincolnshire Local History Society: Industrial History Group)

Westcott, N. 'The East African Sisal Industry 1929-1948', *Journal of African History, 25. (1984)* p.445-461

Wildman, E. Hemp Industry of the Philippines, (*Harper's Weekly, Vol. 44, 1900*)

Wright, N.R. *History of Lincolnshire Volume XI. Lincolnshire Towns and Industry* (12 Vols, History of Lincolnshire committee, 1978) Vol. XI.

Wrightman, C. *More than Munitions: Women, work and the engineering industries, 1900-1950* (Longman, 1989)

Wrigley, E.A. and Schofield, R.S. *The Population History of England, 1541-1871. A Reconstruction.* (Cambridge University Press, 1989)